Quod scriptura, non iubet vetat

The Latin translates, "What is not commanded in scripture, is forbidden:'

On the Cover: Baptists rejoice to hold in common with other evangelicals the main principles of the orthodox Christian faith. However, there are points of difference and these differences are significant. In fact, because these differences arise out of God's revealed will, they are of vital importance. Hence, the barriers of separation between Baptists and others can hardly be considered a trifling matter. To suppose that Baptists are kept apart solely by their views on Baptism or the Lord's Supper is a regrettable misunderstanding. Baptists hold views which distinguish them from Catholics, Congregationalists, Episcopalians, Lutherans, Methodists, Pentecostals, and Presbyterians, and the differences are so great as not only to justify, but to demand, the separate denominational existence of Baptists. Some people think Baptists ought not teach and emphasize their differences but as E.J. Forrester stated in 1893, "Any denomination that has views which justify its separate existence, is bound to promulgate those views. If those views are of sufficient importance to justify a separate existence, they are important enough to create a duty for their promulgation ... the very same reasons which justify the separate existence of any denomination make it the duty of that denomination to teach the distinctive doctrines upon which its separate existence rests." If Baptists have a right to a separate denominational life, it is their duty to propagate their distinctive principles, without which their separate life cannot be justified or maintained.

Many among today's professing Baptists have an agenda to revise the Baptist distinctives and redefine what it means to be a Baptist. Others don't understand why it even matters. The books being reproduced in the *Baptist Distinctives Series* are republished in order that Baptists from the past may state, explain and defend the primary Baptist distinctives as they understood them. It is hoped that this Series will provide a more thorough historical perspective on what it means to be distinctively Baptist.

The Lord Jesus Christ asked, *"And why call ye me, Lord, Lord, and do not the things which I say?"* (Luke 6:46). The immediate context surrounding this question explains what it means to be a true disciple of Christ. Addressing the same issue, Christ's question is meant to show that a confession of discipleship to the Lord Jesus Christ is inconsistent and untrue if it is not accompanied with a corresponding submission to His authoritative commands. Christ's question teaches us that a true recognition of His authority as Lord inevitably includes a submission to the authority of His Word. Hence, with this question Christ has made it forever impossible to separate His authority as King from the authority of His Word. These two principles—the authority of Christ as King and the authority of His Word—are the two most fundamental Baptist distinctives. The first gives rise to the second and out of these two all the other Baptist distinctives emanate. As F.M. Iams wrote in 1894, "Loyalty to Christ as King, manifesting itself in a constant and unswerving obedience to His will as revealed in His written Word, is the real source of all the Baptist distinctives:' In the search for the *primary* Baptist distinctive many have settled on the Lordship of Christ as the most basic distinctive. Strangely, in doing this, some have attempted to separate Christ's Lordship from the authority of Scripture, as if you could embrace Christ's authority without submitting to what He commanded. However, while Christ's Lordship and Kingly authority can be isolated and considered essentially for discussion's sake, we see from Christ's own words in Luke 6:46 that His Lordship is really inseparable from His Word and, with regard to real Christian discipleship, there can be no practical submission to the one without a practical submission to the other.

In the symbol above the Kingly Crown and the Open Bible represent the inseparable truths of Christ's Kingly and Biblical authority. The Crown and Bible graphics are supplemented by three Bible verses (Ecclesiastes 8:4, Matthew 28:18-20, and Luke 6:46) that reiterate and reinforce the inextricable connection between the authority of Christ as King and the authority of His Word. The truths symbolized by these components are further emphasized by the Latin quotation - *quod scriptura, non iubet vetat*— i.e., "What is not commanded in scripture, is forbidden:' This Latin quote has been considered historically as a summary statement of the regulative principle of Scripture. Together these various symbolic components converge to exhibit the two most foundational Baptist Distinctives out of which all the other Baptist Distinctives arise. Consequently, we have chosen this composite symbol as a logo to represent the primary truths set forth in the *Baptist Distinctives Series*.

CORRECTIVE
CHURCH DISCIPLINE

PATRICK HUES MELL
1814-1888

CORRECTIVE CHURCH DISCIPLINE:

WITH A

DEVELOPMENT OF THE SCRIPTURAL PRINCIPLES
UPON WHICH IT IS BASED.

BY

P. H. MELL, D.D.

PROFESSOR IN THE UNIVERSITY OF GEORGIA, AUTHOR OF "BAPTISM IN
ITS MODE AND SUBJECTS," "SAINTS' PERSEVERENCE."

With a Biographical Sketch of the Author by John Franklin Jones

CHARLESTON, S.C.:
SOUTHERN BAPTIST PUBLICATION SOCIETY
J.J. TOON, FINCIAL SECRETARY.
MACON: GA. B.B. & C. SOCIETY....SELMA: B.B. & BOOK
DEPOSITORY.
RICHMOND: T.J. STARKE.
1860

The Baptist Standard Bearer, Inc.
NUMBER ONE IRON OAKS DRIVE • PARIS, ARKANSAS 72855

Thou hast given a *standard* to them that fear thee;
that it may be displayed because of the truth.
-- *Psalm 60:4*

Reprinted 2006

by

THE BAPTIST STANDARD BEARER, INC.
No. 1 Iron Oaks Drive
Paris, Arkansas 72855
(479) 963-3831

THE WALDENSIAN EMBLEM
lux lucet in tenebris
"The Light Shineth in the Darkness"

ISBN# 1579786405

TO THE

Baird's Baptist Church and Congregation,

IN OGLETHORPE COUNTY, GEORGIA,

This Volume

IS RESPECTFULLY DEDICATED BY THEIR AFFECTIONATE

PASTOR.

PREFACE.

The views which are presented in the following pages are such as have been held by the Baptist churches from time immemorial. The Author attempts to do no more than to exhibit the sentiments of our Fathers, and to defend them by showing that they are sustained by the Scriptures. It is not asserted, however, that in no instance have the principles herein set forth been departed from. In times of excitement, when party spirit ran high, or personal resentment swayed men's minds, revolutionary measures have been resorted to in some few of our churches, and these principles have been trampled under foot. Such irregularities have never failed to be disastrous to those who perpetrated them, and their influence upon the cause of Christ has been only evil, and that continually. One of the unhappy effects is that they are taken as precedents by those who are not well informed, and quoted as instances of Baptist usage.

There has been no time in our history, perhaps, when such irregularities could be more easily propagated, if quoted by an influential man, than at the present. In the extraordinary progress of scriptural sentiments on the subject of gospel ordinances, multitudes in this country have been introduced, within a few years, into our churches from Pedobaptist organizations, who are but partially indoctrinated in those opinions which make us a peculiar people. Yielding to the force of the argument on the subject of Baptism, and instructed no further, they have brought into our churches confused notions of church polity, or have even retained undisturbed the views which obtained in the communions they have left. While we cordially welcome these brethren to our ranks, we should see to it that they are instructed in the way of the Lord more perfectly. Should this unpretending little essay have any influence to this end, and tend in any degree to bind the churches to the scriptural sentiments of the Fathers, its author will be more than compensated for his labor.

UNIVERSITY OF GEORGIA,
   March 20, 1860.

CONTENTS.

CHAPTER I.

INTRODUCTION.

	PAGE
1. None but converted persons authorized to be members	7
2. Churches liable to disorders	7
3. The Saviour prescribes the remedies	8

DIFFERENT KINDS OF OFFENCES.

Two kinds—public and private.. 8

PRIVATE OFFENCES.

1. Not necessarily *secret*... 9
2. Specific character of... 9

PUBLIC OFFENCES.

1. Not necessarily committed *publicly*............................ 10
2. Subdivided into two classes.. 10
   First Class.—Offences against religion and morality... 10
   Second Class.—Offences against the church.............. 11
1. Open opposition to the faith and practice of the church.. 11
2. Refusing to attend the meetings of............................... 12
3. Rebellion against its lawful authority............................ 13
4. Attempts to produce schism... 14
   Definitions of the two kinds of offence......................... 14

MIXED OFFENCES.

The two kinds sometimes blended together....................... 15

CHAPTER II.

THE TREATMENT OF THE TWO KINDS OF OFFENCE.

Private offences.. 16
1. First step. *Go* to him... 16

		PAGE
2. *Obj.*—He is an unscrupulous man		16
3. The Saviour's directions to be implicitly obeyed		17
4. Second step. Tell *him* his fault		17
5. Evils attendant upon a resort to the newspapers		17
6. Unsatisfactory results of such resort		20
7. Reasons why the offender should be told his faults		20
1. He may have been misconceived		20
2. He may be reclaimed		20
8. Third step. Tell him his fault between him and thee alone		21
9. Four reasons for this		21
10. When a mutual friend may interpose between parties		21
11. Fourth step. Take one or two more		22
12. Reasons for this		22, 23
13. Fifth step. Tell it to the church		24
14. Idea of reclamation implied		24

TREATMENT OF PUBLIC OFFENCES.

1. Gospel steps not to be taken in open immorality 25
2. Public offenders to be summoned before the church 25
   1. Every facility to be afforded him to meet the charge 25
   2. The formality of a court of justice not to be observed 25
   3. Where alone the offender has ground of complaint 26
3. To be promptly expelled when proved guilty of immorality 26
4. Is the first instance of intoxication to be an exception? 27
   Should be promptly expelled 27
   1. For the sake of public morals and the reputation of the church 27
   2. For his own good 28
   3. As a warning to others 29
5. *Obj.*—Do not the Scriptures say, if he confess, we should forgive? 29
6. They refer exclusively to private offences 29

MIXED OFFENCES.

1. The course to be pursued in 29
2. To be treated as public offences 31
3. Analogy from legal science 31

CHAPTER III.

QUESTIONS SUGGESTED BY THE PREVIOUS DISCUSSION.

1. What shall be done when the aggrieved attempts to bring in private offences without previous gospel steps? 33
   1. The Moderator to rule him out of order 33
   2. In mixed offences, the complaint to be entertained 33

3. No injury done to the accused if the church differ from him as to the nature of the offence... 34
4. How the complainant is to be treated who violates the Saviour's rule... 36
5. Quotation from Elder J. S. Baker.............................. 36
2. Suppose complainant drops the subject: what then?............. 37
3. Whose duty to arraign a public offender?....................... 37
   Any one can arraign... 37
   1. How to act when there is but one witness.................... 38
   2. In case of a report against a brother........................ 38

CHAPTER IV.

THE FEELINGS AND ACTIONS APPROPRIATE TO A PIOUS MAN WHO HAS BEEN UNJUSTLY ACCUSED.

1. Innocence no infallible protection against unjust accusation...... 40
2. Sometimes the victim of prejudice................................ 40
3. Of malice.. 41
4. Of jealousy and envy.. 42
   What his feelings and deportment............................. 43
1. He submits to the Divine will................................... 43
2. In all proper ways defends himself.............................. 43
3. Does not indulge in the spirit of his persecutors, nor resort to the means employed by them....................................... 44
4. Seeks the interest of the church and of the cause of Christ....... 46

CHAPTER V.

WHAT IS "THE CHURCH," TO WHICH THE NEW TESTAMENT GIVES JURISDICTION OVER OFFENCES?

1. The word "church" used in two senses........................... 48
   First. The church universal.................................. 48
   1. The meaning of *ecclesia* in this connection.................. 49
   2. The constituents of this assembly............................ 49
   3. This not the body to whom offences are referred............. 50
   4. The Baptist denomination and the church universal not synonymous... 50
      (1) Some in the Baptist denomination may not have been converted... 50
      (2) Many who have been saved have not belonged to the Baptist denomination....................................... 50
      (3) The use of the word "church" in this sense not admissible.. 51
      (4) Such a body destitute of organization..................... 52

	PAGE
5. Pertinence of the term as applied to the church universal	53
Second. The word "church" applied to a local body	53
1. Composed of those immersed upon a profession of faith	53
2. This the body to whom jurisdiction over offences is given	54

CHAPTER VI.

THE RELATION THE PASTOR SUSTAINS TO CORRECTIVE DISCIPLINE.

1. The importance of the question	55
2. Answered—	
(1) Upon the supposition that the pastor is himself involved	55
(2) Supposing him to be free from entanglement	56
3. His duty in private dealing	56
1. Should endeavor by his ministry to prevent variance	56
2. Should see that private dealing be introduced scripturally	57
3. Should maintain strict neutrality between the parties	57
4. Should bring the pulpit to bear—	
To prevent the formation of parties	57
To make those at variance tired of their relations	58
4. The relation he sustains to cases of public dealing	59
Same principles hold good	59

CHAPTER VII.

DEDUCTIONS FROM PREVIOUS PRINCIPLES—SOVEREIGNTY AND INDEPENDENCE.

Deduction 1. Local churches have exclusive jurisdiction over their members	62
1. Appeal to be made only to the New Testament	62
1. The Saviour *gave* such jurisdiction	62
2. Paul *acknowledges* it	62
3. A church *commended* for exercising it	63
4. Churches *condemned* for not exercising it	63
2. Every church has supreme jurisdiction over its members	64
3. Objection to the use of the term "sovereign"	64
4. Answered—1. The term is apposite to convey the idea	64
2. The idea shown to be scriptural	65
3. Difference between sovereignty and independence	67
5. *Question* 1.—May a member refuse to be tried?	68
Answer.—No way to escape a trial	68

		PAGE
6.	*Quest.* 2.—Suppose he does actually refuse.......................	68
	Ans.—This of itself sufficient ground of expulsion..................	68
7.	*Quest.* 3.—Suppose the arraigned differs from the church as to the kind of offence, &c................	69
	1. The church the only judge of the law and the fact..........	69
	2. After the arraigned raises the point of order, he is free from responsibility....................	70
8.	*Quest.* 4.—Does not a church that rejects the law in Matt. xviii. cease to be a church?........	70
	1. The true case stated..............................	70
	2. The plea upon the principle that an error annihilates a church.............................	71
	3. Shown not to be sustained by the Scriptures................	71
9.	The arraigned not to be the judge in his own case.................	73
10.	Quotation from Elder J. S. Baker..............................	73
11.	Additional argument in favor of sovereignty........................	75
12.	The church has executive authority..............................	76
13.	*Quest.* 1.—May a church expel by majority?.........................	76
14.	Unanimity desirable..	76
	1. Means adopted by some churches to secure unanimity....	76
	2. This implies that the majority must rule.....................	76
15.	Arguments to show that a majority can expel......................	77
	Quotation from Elder J. S. Baker on the point.....................	78
16.	*Quest.* 2.—May a minority never unchurch the majority?.........	78
17.	Answered in the affirmative.....................................	79
	1. Shown on what principle....................................	79
	2. Not applicable to a case of discipline........................	80
18.	Can an arraigned man and his supporters, the minority, unchurch?.................	80
	Shown that on this principle no one of adroitness can be tried............	80
19.	If the majority disregard the law in Matt. xviii., can the minority unchurch?.......	81
	1. To *mistake* the nature of the offence is not to "disregard" the law.............	81
	2. To unintentionally misapply the law, is not to "disregard" it........	82
	3. What alone is a disregard.....................................	82
20.	A minority thus attempting to shield one arraigned should be excommunicated...................	83

CHAPTER VIII.

CHURCH SOVEREIGNTY (*continued*)—TRIAL OF MINISTERS.

1.	Can a minority be tried without Presbytery or Council?...........	84
	1. Shown that they can be................................	84
	2. Writers not all agreed	84

		PAGE
2. No passage in the Bible, in direct terms, prescribes a Presbytery		84
3. Paul *directs* the Galatians to expel false ministers		85
4. Christ praises the Ephesians for expelling false apostles		86
5. Peter acknowledged the jurisdiction of his church over him		86
6. *Objection.*—The ministry was conferred by a Presbytery, &c.		87
7. Preliminary inquiry		87
8. What is a minister?		87
1. The prerogative to preach not peculiar to him		87
2. His prerogative to administer the ordinances		88
9. What is ordination?		88
1. It does not impart any grace or qualification		88
2. Not designed to *authorize* him to preach		89
3. A solemn public recognition		90
10. What relation does a Presbytery bear to ordination?		90
(1) Meaning of Presbytery		90
(2) Different custom in the Northern States		90
(3) In what liable to misconstruction, and in what a corrective		90
11. Two designs in the use of a Presbytery or Council		91
12. Return to the objection		93
13. The Presbytery does not confer the office or make the minister		93
1. It does not take the same power to unmake as to make		93
2. God alone can unmake		94
3. He does interpose by conferring upon the church delegated sovereignty		94
14. *Obj.* 2.—A Presbytery was necessary to give confidence: the same necessary to withdraw it		94
1. More needed to prove ministerial qualification than to detect crime		94
2. A church competent to pass upon a charge of crime		95
15. *Obj.* 3.—To try without a Presbytery implies the right to ordain without		95
1. A church can ordain, though inexpedient		95
2. Ordination a *testimony*		96
3. Not influential without a Presbytery		96
16. The church does not ordain for herself, nor does the Council		97
17. *Obj.* 4.—One ought to be tried by his peers		97
18. The members of the church the minister's peers		97
19. Ministers subject to the churches		98
20. A church *may* call in a Council		98

CHAPTER IX.

DEDUCTIONS (*continued*)—CHURCH INDEPENDENCE—ASSOCIATIONS AND COUNCILS.

1. The decision of the church is final	99
2. Incautious admission	99

		PAGE
3.	The New Testament not silent on the subjects of excommunicating..	100
4.	*Precepts*, in two respects..	100
5.	Directions as to the disposition to be made of the incorrigible...	100
6.	Directions as to our feelings and deportment toward the excommunicated..	101
7.	Scripture *example*..	102
8.	General principles forbid one church to receive the expelled of another..	104
	1. The subordination of the church to Christ........................	104
	2. Every church constituted independent............................	104
	Reception and expulsion not commensurate nor correlative..	107
	Church independence illustrated by a circuit court......	108
	3. Church union...	109
9.	Three kinds of plea by way of objection....................................	110
10.	The plea explanatory..	110
	1st. You do restore to fellowship, or Christian union is destroyed..	111
	2d. Your act would be an interference................................	111
11.	The plea from expediency...	111
	Ans.—The remedy proposed will introduce a greater evil than it corrects...	112
12.	Plea from exceptional cases, Masons, anti-missionaries, &c......	114
	1. One joins the Masons, impelled not by conscience, but by motives of expediency...	114
	2. One becomes a missionary conscientiously.....................	114
	1. Duty of a church-member to seek the harmony of his church..	115
	No necessity for one to allow himself to be expelled for being a Mason..	116
	No excommunicate to be received unless fellowship be withdrawn from the church expelling..............	116
	2. Christian union not affected when one is received who has been expelled for being a missionary..................	118
13.	*Quest.* 1.—Can one expelled apply to his Association or to a Council?...	118
	1. The Scriptures know nothing of Associations and Councils..	118
	The germ of Associations and Councils not to be found in the meeting in Jerusalem......................................	118
	2. Associations of modern date..	120
	How they can be useful...	120
	How they can be perverted..	120
	3. Council, when useful...	121
	Mere advisory bodies called into existence by the church..	122
14.	*Quest.* 2.—May not churches err?..	122
	The way in which they are most likely to err...................	122

CONTENTS.

15. *Quest.* 3.—What remedy has one unjustly expelled?............... 123
    Ans.—None, excepting from the church expelling.................. 123
16. Uses to which he may put his expulsion............................... 123
    1. He may submit humbly to the will of God................... 123
    2. He may suffer as a martyr.. 124
    3. He may wait patiently, and by a well-ordered life and godly conversation disabuse the minds of his brethren 124
    4. He may find consolation in the fact that expulsion from the church is not expulsion from the kingdom of heaven.. 125

CORRECTIVE CHURCH DISCIPLINE.

CHAPTER I.

It is the Saviour's will of precept that the constituents of His churches shall be regenerated persons. He authorizes none to receive the ordinance of Baptism, and to have a lot among His visible people, but those who believe with the heart that He is the Son of God. His churches, however, are not composed of perfect beings. Men of passions and infirmities, of prejudices and defective knowledge,—frequently of discordant tastes and conflicting worldly interests,—are congregated together, and organized into visible local societies. In these circumstances, it must needs be that offences come. The influence of the grace of God, and the precepts of the gospel, serve to counteract this tendency; but it is never impossible for the flesh to get, for the time, the mastery of the spirit, and produce alienation among individuals, or discord in communities where brotherly love, order, and harmony usually prevail.

The Great Lawgiver in Zion recognizes the possibility of the action of disturbing elements, and has left His people in no doubt as to the remedy to be applied in every instance. He has not left us to legislate on the subject, nor to resort to expedients to meet cases as they arise, but Himself has classified offences, and prescribed the course to be pursued in every case. It only remains for us to perceive clearly the Divine discrimination, and to carry out implicitly the Divine prescription.

What then is the inspired classification of offences? —and what, under the classification, is the course of treatment prescribed by Infinite Wisdom?

The Scriptures cite us to but two kinds of offence. Matt. xviii. 15 points out the one kind, where the object of the offence is an individual, —"If thy brother trespass against thee;" and 1 Cor. v. to the second kind, where the object of the offence is either public morals or the Church. The former of these is usually characterized by the term PRIVATE, and the latter by the term PUBLIC. The use of these terms will be retained in this essay, though they are each liable to some ambiguity of meaning. PERSONAL is employed by some in preference to "Private;" but neither term is exactly suited to the case, since *private* may be understood in the sense of *secret;* and *personal* is not necessarily in antithesis to *public.* Nor is the term *public* more happy in conveying the idea intended, since it may be understood in

[marginal note: Different kinds of offence.]

the sense of *ostentatiously—before the world*. If this criticism be repeated in substance, it will be only to warn the reader against a misapprehension of the idea designed to be conveyed.

1. *Private offences.* What are "private offences," as described in Matt. xviii. ?

Ans. 1. Not necessarily *secret* offences. Many "public offences" are committed secretly; as theft, fornication, &c. The thief and the fornicator select the time usually when the friendly darkness will conceal them,—when they confidently trust no eye will detect them. But theft and fornication are not "private" but "public" offences, according to scriptural classification, even though the former may have been committed against a brother. But of this more anon.

Ans. 2. "Private offences," then, *i.e.* those referred to in Matt. xviii., are those that are *personal*, committed exclusively against *individuals;* as when encroachments are made upon individual *rights, interests, or feelings.* A, on the impulse of the moment, accidentally cripples B's stock that have broken into his inclosure, or, through mistake, makes encroachments upon his territory, or speaks harshly or disparagingly of him, or accosts him in a cold and repulsive manner, or refuses to speak to him at all: —these are a very few examples of an offence specific in character, but endless in combination and manifestation. The *specific character* is that *the act* is

B   2*

not a crime against religion and morality, and *the object of the act* is a brother.

2. *Public offences.* What are "public offences"?
Ans. 1. Not necessarily those that are committed *publicly* and *ostentatiously*. One church-member may publicly and ostentatiously refuse to speak to another, and in other ways unjustly treat him with contempt. But, as has been seen above, this is not a "public" but a "private" offence, since the object of it is exclusively an individual. Those who perpetrate "public offences" more frequently, though not always, try to conceal them under the veil of secrecy.

Ans. 2. "Public offences" may be subdivided into two classes:—(1.) Where they are crimes exclusively against religion and morality; and, (2,) where they are offences against the Church in its organized capacity.

(1.) A crime is committed against religion and morality exclusively when the offence has no individual or body of individuals for its object; but when it is incited for the gratification of a depraved taste or for the indulgence of a corrupt propensity; as drunkenness, profanity, lewdness, falsehood, &c.,— the last not perpetrated against an individual. Here the offences are crimes not against men, but against God. The drunken church-member, *in the mere fact that he is drunk,* infringes upon no brother's personal rights, tramples upon no brother's individual feelings, and damages no brother's personal individual interests. This is not the intention, this is not the result. The only object may have been to gratify a depraved appetite. He is a "public offender," (1st,) because he has committed a grievous offence, and (2d) because the object affected by the offence is not an individual, but public gospel morality and the cause of Christ.

(2.) Transgressions committed against the Church in its organized capacity constitute another class of "public offences." The instances of this kind of offence are innumerable, some of which may be given as follows:—

(1.) When a member of the Church openly renounces its doctrines of faith, and engages in an active and uncompromising effort to subvert them,—when he denounces its practice of restricted communion, gives notice that he means to disregard it, and carries the annunciation into effect by the overt act,—he is a public offender. Here the object affected by the offender's act is not the individual members of the Church, but the Church in its organized capacity. Let not this citation, however, be misunderstood. No reference is made to those who are ignorant of Gospel doctrines, or who even have doubts as to the Scriptural character of those held by the Church. A gospel church is not a circle of doctrinal proficients, but a school for learners, where those who are acquainted only with the alphabet of the gospel—with the first principles of the doctrine of Christ—may receive instruction, and know as they follow on to know the Lord. The only qualification for admission into a gospel church is repentance towards God, and faith in the Lord Jesus Christ. There are, doubtless, multitudes in the churches who know nothing of the profound doctrines of grace, or even have misgivings as to the correctness of the interpretations put upon them, who are yet guilty of no offence, and members in good standing. Reference is had to those, solely, who declare open war against the doctrines and practices of the Church and engage in active efforts to subvert and destroy them. The Church is bound to hold these as "public offenders;" and if there is to be any difference in the treatment of their case and in that of other public offenders, it is to be found in the injunction, "A man that is a heretic, *after the first and second admonition*, reject." Tit. iii. 10.

(2.) Refusal, after admonition, to attend upon the stated conference-meetings of the Church, is a "public offence." Here, again, the object affected by the act is not the individual members of the Church, but the Church in its organized capacity. Nor is the act an infraction of the public rules of gospel morality, excepting in so far as it may be a violation of the member's vows when he entered into the Church. Nowhere in the Scriptures is a rule in so many words, (such as not a few of our churches have passed,) requiring attendance of members at such an hour of such a day on conference-meetings. According to the Scriptures, there is necessarily no immorality in an absence from any place on any Saturday in the month; yet our churches, acting within lawful limits, have passed such a rule, and their members have pledged themselves to abide by it. Nothing is more common than for churches to expel members, after admonition, for non-attendance upon conference-meetings. Why? What is the nature of the offence? Not "private," certainly; because no infringement has been made upon individual rights, interests, or feelings; not public, in the sense that a crime, in the nature of things, has been committed against gospel morality, for simple absence from any time and place contains essentially no moral character; but a "public offence," because it is committed against the authority of the Church, which the member is bound and pledged to regard.

(3.) Rebellion against the lawful authority of the Church—a refusal to heed its citations, or, in other ways, a denial of its lawful jurisdiction over him—is, on the part of the member, a "public offence." He neglects to hear the Church, and, if he persists,—by Divine direction,—is to be considered by her in the light of a "heathen man and a publican." Every consideration drawn from the Scriptures, and from the Church's sense of duty to herself and to the cause of Christ, requires her to cut off from herself a member in a state of open rebellion. But the offender may not have trespassed at all upon individuals, and he may have been guilty of no gross offence against morals,—*i.e.* such as is incited by depraved tastes and corrupt propensities. He is, nevertheless, guilty of a public offence, since he is found arrayed in open rebellion against the authority with which Christ has invested His Church.

(4) It is a "public offence to attempt to make divisions and disturbances in a church. A schismatic, one who factiously distracts the Church, and threatens to divide it, the Church is expressly commanded to excommunicate. 'Mark them who cause divisions and offences, contrary to the doctrine which ye have learned, and avoid them.' Rom. xvi. 17, 18. Here, again, the act, because perpetrated against the Church in its organized capacity, authority, and interests, is a public offence." These are but a few of the many instances that may be cited.

The following, then, are the conclusions to which we arrive:—

1. A "Private Offence" is one in which *the act* is not essentially a crime against religion and morality, and *the object affected by it* is a brother.

2. A "Public Offence" is one in which *the act* is essentially a crime against religion or morality, or *the object of it* the Church in its organized capacity.

But it is sometimes the case that these two kinds

of offence are so blended together as to seem to constitute a third class. It is from this combination that nearly all the difficulty originates in the treatment. Further on, it will be shown that these do not constitute a distinct class. For the sake of convenience, however, they will be termed here *mixed offences.* Where *the act* is essentially a crime against religion and morality, and the *object affected by it* is a brother, we have both offences in combination. The following may be given as examples of this:—*Willful* and *malicious slander* against a brother; *profane* denunciation of him; *theft* from him; *fraud* perpetrated upon him; *seduction;* personal violent assault upon him, with fist, bludgeon, or horsewhip, violent and libelous publication of him in the newspapers, or by advertisement set up in conspicuous places. These are a few of many examples which may be given. Falsehood, profanity, theft, fraud, seduction, a breach of the peace by personal violence or libelous publication, are offences against religion and morality, though they may be perpetrated against members of the Church.

3. *Mixed offences.*

CHAPTER II.

THE TREATMENT OF THE TWO KINDS OF OFFENCE.

<small>1. *Private offences.*</small> In the treatment of "private offences," the Saviour, in Matt. xviii., gives the course to be pursued, commonly called "Gospel steps:" "Go and tell him his fault between him and thee alone." 1st. *Go to him* and seek a private interview. Observe, he does not say, address him a note, or employ a committee of friends to negotiate with "seconds," who may represent your antagonist as men of the world do in their so-called "affairs of honor." Submit the case to no second hands, but "go" yourself, and see your offending brother face to face.

<small>*Objection.*—But it may be objected, "I have to deal with an unscrupulous man, who will pervert my words, or otherwise misrepresent our interview to my injury. For my own protection, therefore, I must have our mutual communications in writing, or, at least, secure the presence of witnesses who may correct his misrepresentations."</small>

The amount of this is, you must do evil that good may come,—or, at least, that evil may be avoided. You have too little faith in the prescriptions of Christ, and must substitute expedients of your own.

But, unfortunately for you, in the very unlawful precautions you use, you place yourself completely in the power of him whom you characterize as a designing man. I grant you that if your antagonist (for that is the correct term, under the present aspect) does take advantage of your disobedience and indiscretion, and use them for your injury, he goes far to prove himself the unscrupulous and wicked man you fear he is; but this development is of no advantage to you, since it does not atone for your disobedience, nor make you any the less completely in his power. You lack confidence in the prescriptions of Christ, and propose to substitute precautions and expedients of your own, and the Master may suffer you to be involved in a long train of inconsistencies, embarrassments, and suffering. The first direction, then, to be observed, is, seek an interview with your offending brother face to face.

Tell him. Not blaze it abroad in the newspapers, nor growl about it in the presence of others; but go and tell HIM his fault, in the spirit of meekness. It is a question whether our religious newspaper press has not been used too much of late to produce and to aggravate personal differences between brethren. If the editors have themselves not been the guilty parties, have they not been too ready to yield their columns to excited persons, who have real or fancied grievances to allege

2. "*Tell him his fault.*"

against their brethren? The first that is heard, even by the alleged offender, of the thing complained of, is contained, perhaps, in a newspaper article. In this, by innuendo, by insinuation, or by statement in detail, *the public* are told how greatly the writer has suffered in his person, his rights, his interests, or his feelings, by the action or the words of the real or fancied aggressor. The latter is held up as a very bad man, and the public are impliedly called upon to condemn him. If the one assailed possesses a similar spirit, rejoinder is to be expected in the public newspapers: the gauntlet thrown down is promptly to be taken up. The appeal now on both sides is to *the public;* and the effort of each is to array as partisans as many of that public as he can. This is especially true if the parties at variance are men of influence and equally matched in strength. At first but one newspaper column may be wheeled into hostile position. The war begins with a single gun on either side. Only one embrasure of the newspaper battery opens for the protrusion of the hostile ordnance. But, as the hot shot and shell, the grape and canister, tell with reciprocal execution, the excitement and the rancor rise in intensity, until progressively the whole battery is unmasked and every gun is plied with deadly execution. Begrimed with smoke and distorted by passion, the countenances of the combatants bear no longer the lineaments of followers of the Prince of

Peace. The din and uproar drown the gentle voice of conscience and the sweet monitions of the Holy Spirit, while the sulphureous smoke, charged with an odor from the world beneath, poisons the upper air and shuts out from the combatants the blessed light of heaven.

This, however, is but the beginning of the fray, the distant cannonading with which the conflict opens. Forces must be raised, and resources gathered, that the issue may be decided in a pitched battle, by a hand-to-hand engagement. To attract recruits and rally forces to the standard, each plants himself upon some great principle dear to people's hearts, which, if you would believe him, he has been set to defend, and which must stand or fall with him; or the cry is raised that the religious party he represents is to be trampled in the dust in his person. The slogan of party catches the ear of the heated, the restless, and the ultra; and the cry of "principles in danger" arouses the quiet and conservative like the sound of the fire-bell at night. Vast armaments are gathered, and stand face to face in hostile force. And what then? A religious Solferino is fought. The battle rages in the midst of the cries and imprecations and slaughter of BRETHREN. And when the reputed victor, in the midst of his exhausted forces, surrounded by the dying and the dead, comes to sum up the result, it is only to find himself arrested by obstacles he cannot force, and glad to enter into a Villa Franca truce, which will end in nothing but protracted negotiations and endless complications. *The leaders, drifted whither they did not intend, invariably fail in their purposes;* while the people, their adherents, with feelings embittered and brotherly love destroyed, find their ancient landmarks obliterated, and their cherished institutions wellnigh subverted and destroyed; a-n-d—that is all!

How different, however, are the process and result when the Saviour's directions are observed!

"Tell HIM his fault," because,—

1. You may have misconceived him through misapprehension or misrepresentations. Your brother may be able to DISAVOW, or, if he acknowledges, to EXPLAIN, and thus remove all complaint.

2. You may thus be able to RECLAIM him. When your brother trespasses against you, he sins against God also, and against his own soul. How much more noble, then, is it for you, keeping your own heart right, to reform and "gain," than to come off victorious over your brother in mortal conflict! "Brethren, if a man be overtaken in a fault, ye which are spiritual restore such an one in the spirit of meekness, considering thyself lest thou also be tempted." "Brethren, if any of you do err from the truth, and one convert him, let him know that he which converteth the sinner from the error of his

way, shall save a soul from death, and shall hide a multitude of sins." James v. 19, 20.

"Tell him his fault *between him and thee alone.*"

1. If you go in the first instance accompanied by others, you may seem to have summarily decided against the offender, without giving him a hearing, and thus excite in him a spirit of *independence* and *defiance.*

2. You may seem to have no confidence in his capacity to do right, and thus rouse his *resentment.*

3. Accompanied by others, you may seem to have entered into a conspiracy against him. It may appear that you are approaching him systematically as an enemy to entangle and expose him, and thus put him on the *defensive.* If he is cautious and prudent, you make him wary, but not the less an antagonist; if he is fiery and impulsive, you make him aggravate the difficulty by defiance and *wrath.*

4. You may seem to be desirous to humble him by making him succumb and confess his fault before witnesses, and thus touch his *pride.*

The great object is to "gain your brother:" therefore, make the attempt first by yourself.

Question.—"But may a mutual friend in no instance make the effort to bring parties mutually at variance together, and induce them to talk about their points of difference in his presence?"

Ans.—To this it is answered, that it is perfectly legitimate for a mutual friend to bring variant parties together. And, by so doing, it is often the case that much good is accomplished.

But you observe that the question proposes a case very different from that under discussion. You speak of those who are *mutual* trespassers,—who are equally at variance, and therefore both wrong. But the question under discussion relates to a case where only one is a trespasser, while the other is as yet free from blame. Our discussion relates to the duty of the one who, yet free from wrong in act or feeling, has been trespassed upon by his brother. The duty of such is to keep right himself, and to do all in his power to recover his erring brother.

After all the disinterested efforts made by yourself, the offender may remain incorrigible. What then? Become disgusted with him?—leave him to himself, and treat him ever thereafter as an enemy? Bring him before the Church? No. One step more remains to be taken.

4. "*Take with thee one or two more*,"—not partisans or enemies, but those in whom the offender has confidence:

1st, That they may be arbitrators between you. If, after they hear him, they are satisfied that he is wrong, they can tell him so, and add their influence to yours to bring him right.

2d, If he is incorrigible, they may be witnesses for you in the next step you may have to take.

The Saviour designs that His people shall not be

at variance. It is His revealed will that brotherly love shall continue among them, and that they shall be of one heart and of one mind. If, however, variance should arise, He requires the parties to settle it privately between themselves; and He gives directions which, if followed implicitly, and the heart of each is right, will lead to the desired result.

He requires you to settle your difficulties privately between yourselves, because,—

1. In no other way can they be settled to the mutual, hearty satisfaction of both parties. Any other method of settlement will consist either in the condemnation of one or both of the parties, or in a compromise between them which will satisfy neither.

2. He would save His cause from the reproach of brethren publicly worrying and devouring one another.

3. He would save His churches from the adjudication of personal difficulties between their members; so that they may never be the arena for personal strife, nor the field of battle for conflicting hosts.

4. But, if the offender continues incorrigible, He has provided, in the directions He gives, not only for the safety of the innocent and the punishment of the incorrigibly guilty, but for the peace and unanimity of His Church, which is to be the tribunal in the last resort. "In the mouth of two or three witnesses every word may be established." By their testimony, the "one or two" disinterested brethren may

afford protection to the innocent and light to the Church, so that it may act with unanimity and unerring certainty.

If all the efforts made by the aggrieved *alone*, and in conjunction with the "one or two" disinterested brethren, fail, the case assumes the character of a "public offence;" and the last step is to be taken by the offended.

5. "*Tell it to the Church.*" Of course, in the spirit of meekness, with the hope and prayer still that the offender may be reclaimed. This idea of reclamation is distinctly implied in the words following:—"If he *neglect to hear* the Church, let him be to thee as a heathen man and a publican." He may *not* neglect to hear the Church. What then? Even then, though he has been almost lost, you may "gain your brother." It is imperative upon the Church, when a question of mere personal variance, involving no immorality, is brought before it, to attempt in the first instance to reclaim the offender. It is her duty to examine into the facts, and to use her arguments and moral force to bring him to a sense of his wrong and to a reparation *of it*. Never, until she *speaks* to him and he deliberately and persistently "neglects to hear," is she, by the ultimate resort, to make him bear to her the relation of "a heathen man and a publican."

Of the effects of excommunication by a church, more will be said anon.

How should public offences be treated? When one has been guilty of open immorality, shall "gospel steps" be taken? Is it demanded that a thief, or a drunkard, or a debauchee, should be approached first in private, and then in company with one or two others, before he is arraigned in presence of the Church? Certainly not; for no private reparation can atone for, or counteract the effects of, immoralities.

Treatment of public offences.

1. If he does not bring the matter up himself, he should be cited to appear and answer to the charge. In this arraignment, he should have every facility to meet the charge against him; for it does by no means follow that every one is guilty who has been accused. No one should be condemned without a hearing; and, to have a hearing, he must be in possession of all the counts of the indictment against him. He must have the privilege of confronting the witnesses, and of sifting the testimony against him, that he may be able to speak effectively and to the point in his own behalf. It is not meant, though, to be asserted here that a church should go through with all the formality observed by a court of justice, but simply that no one should be forced to a trial until he becomes fully informed of all the charges and has an opportunity to sift the evidence relied upon to convict. Excepting in extreme and very complicated cases, no written documents need

be employed in the citation and trial. The arraigned may hear the charge for the first time as it may be announced orally, or read from the clerk's record, in open conference. If he pleads not guilty, and desires time to prepare himself for the trial, all reasonable indulgence should be granted, and nothing pertaining to the case should be withheld from him.

It goes far, however, to show conscious guilt, if a church-member arraigned endeavors to quash proceedings by the plea that he had not been served with written processes. *Not until he asks for information, and for the postponement of his trial*, and is refused by the Church, has he any ground of complaint. Church-trials are designed not only to convict the guilty, but to clear the innocent who have been accused. An innocent man, then, so far from trying to embarrass the action of the Church in the premises, will do all in his power to facilitate such action. It is for the interest of the innocent that the Church promptly and thoroughly investigate the charges against him, that his innocence *may appear*, and that the confidence of his brethren and of the world may be restored to him. And it goes far to prove, if not his guilt, at least a heart not right, for the accused to take offence at the arraignment or ascribe it to conspiracy against him.

2. If the arraigned is proved to be guilty of a gross offence against religion and morality, he should be at once, and without delay, expelled. "Put

away from among yourselves that wicked person." 1 Cor. v. 13. All will grant that this conclusion is correct in regard to such offenses as murder, fornication, theft, &c.; but they do not see that *railing*, covetousness, drunkenness, and extortion may not be dealt with more gently, and forgiven upon repentance and confession. The Apostle Paul, however, places them all in the same category with fornication, and prescribes the same treatment to them all in common. "But now I have written unto you not to keep company, if any man that is called a brother be a fornicator, or covetous, or an idolater, or a railer, or a drunkard, or an extortioner; with such an one no not to eat." 1 Cor. v. 11.

It is the opinion of some—and there may be force in it, though not perceived by the present writer—that in the case of drunkenness the first offence may be forgiven on repentance and confession; since in that instance the offender may have been "*overtaken in a fault;*" and that it takes a repetition of the act to show that he is properly a "*drunkard.*" Be this as it may, just so soon as these and other gross crimes are proved upon one that is "called a brother," he should be withdrawn from.

1. For the sake of public morals and the reputation of the Church, she should testify unmistakably. This course would meet with approbation more heartily from no one than from the offender himself, if he is a Christian; for to such the honor of the

Master and the reputation of His Church are dearer than his own good name, or even than life itself. When a confession of sin and a profession of penitence are received as satisfactory, and the offender forgiven, the act may be misunderstood by the world; but when the member is cut off, there is no room to suppose that the Church views the offence as trivial and venial.

2. For the good of the offender himself, he should be excommunicated. If he is not a Christian, he should not be a member of the Church; if he is a Christian, excommunication will not harm him. Corrective discipline, even in its highest censures, is an act of kindness to the offender, and designed not to injure but to reform. Such was the effect of the discipline inflicted upon the incestuous man at Corinth. While undisturbed by his brethren and permitted to go on in sin with impunity, he seemed not to be aware of the enormity of his crime; but after expulsion he is brought to reflection and penitence. So that we find the apostle, who had demanded his exclusion, afterwards, on satisfactory evidence of his repentance and reformation, acting as his intercessor and begging his restoration. "Sufficient to such a man is this punishment which was inflicted of many. So that, contrariwise, ye ought rather to forgive him and comfort him; lest perhaps such a one should be swallowed up with overmuch sorrow.

Wherefore I beseech you that you would confirm your love towards him."

3. As a warning to others, the Church should affix to gross crime unmistakably the mark of its reprobation.

Objection.—But it may be objected, "Do not the Scriptures say, 'If a brother confess his fault we should forgive him'?"

Ans.—To this it is answered, that the injunction refers exclusively to private or personal offences. "Take heed to yourselves: if thy brother trespass against *thee*, rebuke him; and if he repent, forgive him. And if he trespass against *thee* seven times in a day, and seven times in a day turn again to thee, saying, I repent, thou shalt forgive him."

In public offences not involving gross immorality, a milder course may be pursued, and corrective discipline may be successful and complete short of excommunication.

Treatment of mixed offences. What course is to be pursued in mixed offences? When *the act* is a public offence, and the *object affected by it* a brother, is it his duty to take "gospel steps"? When one willfully slanders his brother, or defrauds or steals from him, or violently assaults his person, or libelously publishes him, is he the less a liar, a defrauder, a thief, an infractor of the peace, and a libeler, because his victim happens to be a member of the Church? Suppose these acts had been perpetrated against one not a church-member: would they not have been criminal? Would not the Church have been bound to take cognizance of them? And if so, under what head of offences would she have classed them? If they are crimes against religion and morality when committed against an irreligious man, do they lose their nature when committed against a member of the Church? *Whatever may be counteracted, or removed, or atoned for, so that neither individuals nor the cause may be injured*, can be disposed of by private dealing. But gross public offences, whatever may be their combinations or objects, cannot be disposed of in that way. The brother trespassed upon may be, and doubtless is, under obligations to seek a private interview with the brother who *he believes* has willfully slandered, or defrauded, or stolen from him; since in all these things he may have been mistaken. He may even pursue a like course with one who has horsewhipped or libeled him, and bring them all to confession of their wrong, and to a tender of all the private reparation in their power. But would that relieve the Church from the obligation to discipline its members for the crimes against religion and morality contained in lying, in fraud, in seduction, in theft, in a breach of the peace by personal assault and libel? Nay, if the one trespassed upon in the ways indicated above concludes to take no action in the premises, and to bear his grievances in silence, would the Church, acquainted with the facts, be debarred by this from dealing with its members for lying, fraud, theft, &c.?

The answer to be given, then, to the question at the beginning of the above paragraph, is, If *the act is a gross offence against religion and morality, and the object affected by it* a brother, it is to be dealt with as other gross offences that are purely "public," whether the aggrieved takes "gospel steps" or not.

Thus it will be seen that in "mixed offences" *the nature of the sin* is the basis of its classification, and not merely the object against which it is committed. The "private" feature is merged in and swallowed up by the gross crime which constitutes the act. This is nothing novel. The same classification obtains in legal science Sir Wm. Blackstone, in his Commentaries, book iv. chap. 1, p. 5, says, "Murder is an injury to the life of an individual; but the law of society considers principally the loss which the state sustains by being deprived of a member, and the pernicious example thereby set for others to do the like. Robbery may be considered in the same view : it is an injury to *private* property; but, were that all, a civil satisfaction in damages might atone for it: the *public* mischief is the thing for the prevention of which our laws have made it a capital offence. In these gross and atrocious injuries the private wrong is swallowed up in the public: we seldom hear any mention made of satisfaction to the individual, the satisfaction to the community being so very great. And, indeed, as the public crime is not otherwise avenged than by forfeiture of life and property, it is impossible afterwards to make any reparation for the private wrong; which can only be had from the body or goods of the aggressor." In like manner, in the case of theft, seduction, murder, or other gross crimes, as the offence against religion and morality can in no other way be atoned for than by the expulsion of the offender, it is a matter of no importance, so far as it relates to the question of his continued church-membership, whether or not he renders satisfaction, if possible, to the individual his victim.

And it will be seen, also, that those that for convenience have been termed "mixed" do not constitute a distinct class, but are to be ranged under the head of "public offences" and treated accordingly.

CHAPTER III.

QUESTIONS SUGGESTED BY THE PREVIOUS DISCUSSION.

Question.—1. SUPPOSE the aggrieved attempt to bring strictly *private offences* into the Church without taking "gospel steps:" what should be done?

Ans.—It is the duty of the pastor or other Moderator to inquire whether the Saviour's directions have been followed, and, if he finds that they have not been, he should rule as out of order the introduction of the case. If the pastor should fail to discharge this duty, then it will be competent for any member to raise the point of order, and to appeal from the decision of the chair, if *it* be in violation of the Saviour's rule. And the Church, when thus appealed to, is in duty bound to overrule by vote the decision of its presiding officer. This is said of offences exclusively that are *purely personal*,—when the act is not a crime against religion and morality, and the object affected by it is a brother. In "mixed offences," where the act complained of is a gross immorality,—as theft, slander, seduction, fraud, personal violence, and libel,—it will not be out of order for the Church to entertain the charge though no "gospel steps" have been taken, since, as has been shown, these and the like gross offences against religion and morality are "public offences," though they may have been committed against a church-member.

But it may be asked, "May not the arraigned himself raise the point of order?" Most assuredly. "And if raised by him, how is it to be decided?" By the ruling of the Moderator first, and, if this be appealed from, by the vote of the Church. *And the decision of the Church is final.* "But if *he claims to think* it to be purely a private offence, and that, therefore, the proceedings are premature, is it not a great hardship and injustice to the accused for the Church to entertain the charge?" Assuredly not, *if he is innocent.* In our courts of justice, parties arraigned for crime pick flaws in the indictment, and endeavor to quash the proceedings on technical grounds, when they feel themselves in doubt as to their ability to meet the main issue successfully. But when they are satisfied that they are able to clear their character from aspersion before their fellow citizens, they waive all plea from informality of proceedings, and court a thorough investigation. It would be a great outrage to withhold from an arraigned man the charges alleged against him, or to press him to trial without giving him reasonable time to prepare for it; but a slight mistake in the technical wording of the indictment is neither outrage nor injustice to him,—nor would he avail himself of it to quash proceedings, *unless he felt conscious that he needed such a plea,* and placed a higher estimate upon a mere release from trial than upon his good name and standing among his fellows. In no respect can injustice be done to the accused by what he is pleased to consider a premature entertainment of the charge. He is either guilty or innocent of theft, or fraud, or personal violence, or libel, or other gross crime committed against another, a church-member or not. If guilty, no arraignment *after the commission of that act* can be premature. If innocent, he cannot too soon be afforded an opportunity to free himself from the charge. And when one thus charged strives to divert attention from the indictment, and endeavors to fix it upon some alleged informality, he goes far to show to all discerning persons that he is conscious of an inability to meet the issue; and, to say the least, he excites in their minds a strong suspicion of his guilt.

In another connection the question will be discussed as to how far responsibility attaches to the arraigned when the Church, in the management of his case, treats as "public" that which is purely a "private" case; and what in the premises are his duties to the cause of Christ.

Strictly private offences, however, should be ruled

out of order when attempted to be brought into the Church without previous "gospel steps" resorted to ineffectually. If the complainant, through ignorance, attempts to introduce it, he should be kindly instructed as to his duty. If he acts thus with willful disregard of his obligations, he should be reproved and compelled to follow the Saviour's rule.*

---

* No one has written more discriminatingly and forcibly on Church discipline than Elder Joseph S. Baker. From him the present writer took his first lessons on the subject. Bro. Baker does not seem fully to sustain me in this position, but his views are worthy of consideration. He says:—

"There is one error . . . prevalent in our Churches which should be corrected. We allude to the opinion that a violation of the rule by the aggrieved, in bringing an offender before the Church before he has pursued the course prescribed by the Saviour, relieves the Church from the obligation to deal with the individual thus arraigned before them." After reasoning forcibly against this, he lays down two propositions; the first of which is,

1. "A Church is bound to take cognizance of every manifest violation by its members of any of the laws of Christ's kingdom, with which it becomes acquainted, whether the information of such violation is communicated in regular order or not.

"The reasons for this rule are obvious. The Church is required to set the seal of her disapprobation on every transgression of the law of God. Her obligation to do this is not made to depend, in the slightest degree, upon the means by which she arrives at a knowledge of the transgression; for the character of an offence is not affected in the least by the manner in which it is made known. The magistrate is as much bound to have a band of robbers arrested, when information of their acts of robbery is communicated by one of their own number who has turned a traitor, as when it is communicated by an honest and orderly citizen. And so is the

CORRECTIVE CHURCH DISCIPLINE.

Question.—2. Suppose the complainant drops the subject and takes no further action: what then?

Ans. 1.—If he silently bears his grievance and suppresses all resentment, making it not the occasion of disturbance, his patience and meekness (if he is influenced by these) is commendable; but he is guilty of sin in not obeying his Saviour and attempting to "gain his brother."

Ans. 2.—If the variance continues, the Church may, and is in duty bound to, arraign both parties,—one for failing to follow the instructions of Christ, the other for his trespass; and both for being, by their wrangling, disturbers of the peace.

Question.—3. Whose duty is it to arraign a public offender?

Ans.—Any one who witnessed the act, or has heard the rumor of it, or has felt the effect of it. On no plea of obscurity, or youth, or sex, can church-members excuse themselves for silence and inaction,

---

Church as much bound to notice offences committed, when she receives her intelligence through one who is himself an offender, as when she receives it through the most harmless and exemplary of her members. So long as she is ignorant of the offences committed by her members, she is not chargeable with them; but the moment she is made acquainted with them, if she fails to adopt measures for calling the offenders to account, and for preventing the recurrence of like offences in future, she virtually sanctions those offences, bids the offenders God speed, becomes a partaker of their evil deeds, and renders herself amenable both to God and man."—*Periodical Library,* Vol. I. No. 4 (1847), pp. 262, 263.

while public offenders are wounding Christ in the house of His friends. Nothing said above, though, is designed to condemn those who, on account of obscurity, youth, or sex, prefer to put the facts into the hands of more aged and influential brethren, holding themselves in readiness to act as witnesses when called on.

Caution.—It may, however, in some cases, be best to see the offender first, before you act.

1. You may have been the only one who witnessed the deed. In that case, it would be best to ascertain whether he will acknowledge it. He may, when you arraign him, plead not guilty. Should he do so, and his previous character be unimpeached, you may place yourself and the Church in an embarrassing position. Your charge will be met by his denial; and there will be simply a question of veracity between you. Now, it is not impossible for a charge of gross immorality in overt act to be brought maliciously against an innocent person. Unless, then, you can present corroborating circumstances to sustain your allegation, in the event he will plead not guilty, painful as it may be, you had better remain silent, and wait until the developments of Providence shall further expose him. Instances have been known in which Churches have been compelled to excommunicate both the arraigner and arraigned from not being able to know whether the latter had been guilty or only maliciously slandered, and be-

cause of the irritation caused by the question of veracity. When more than one, however, are able to testify to the fact, or circumstances strongly corroborate the allegation, the offender need not be seen first.

2. By seeing the offender first, he may be induced to bring the matter forward himself, and thus relieve others from an unpleasant and sometimes hazardous duty.

3. In the case of a report to the disadvantage of a brother, it is especially important that you see him first before you act. The report you have heard may not be general rumor, but a falsehood of limited circulation and recent origin. For you to announce this in the public meeting of the Church will be to give it a wider circulation. It is always proper, then, for you first to put your brother in possession of the report circulating to his discredit, and aid him to trace it up to its source. If, after this, the rumor increases, and seems to be well founded, and the brother tries to hush it up,—declining to take any further action in the premises,—it is your duty to name it in the Church, that a committee of investigation may be appointed.

CHAPTER IV.

THE FEELINGS AND ACTIONS APPROPRIATE TO A PIOUS MAN WHO HAS BEEN UNJUSTLY ACCUSED.

The fate of the Saviour of the world is a striking proof that innocence is no infallible protection against unjust accusation and condemnation. From the world the Christian is prepared to expect tribulation; for he that will live godly in Christ Jesus shall suffer persecution; and if they call the master of the house Beelzebub, how much more will they those of his household! But in the Church of God he feels secure. From his brethren, children of the same heavenly Father and subjects of the same divine grace, he expects nothing but brotherly sympathy, encouragement, and protection. But Paul has told us of perils among false brethren; and how often are a man's enemies those of his own household!

It is not impossible for a man of true piety and unexceptionable deportment to find himself, through misapprehension, malice, or jealousy, unjustly arraigned before his brethren.

Sometimes he is the victim of PREJUDICE. His

brethren have been taught in advance to believe him capable of wrong; and his acts, imperfectly understood, and seen through the medium of prejudice, may be so colored and distorted as to seem hideous. Certain causes, acting upon a peculiar nervous constitution, may produce effects in speech and manner that may appear equivocal; or he may be the victim of a train of circumstances which may seem to implicate him in a crime that his soul abhors.

Purity of heart and life is no infallible protection against the machinations and the tongue of MALICE. Nay, this very purity may be the occasion to arouse the vindictiveness of the vile and wicked. A holy life is a standing reproof against their depravity; and, while it deserves to command their respect, it as often excites their resentment. Nor is this feeling confined to the world. Often—with regret it is confessed—do the worldly-minded members of the Church feel resentment against those whose uniform consistency is a constant reproof to their laxity of principles and irregularity of deportment. In times of apostasy and defection from the truth, those who adhere to their principles, and lift up their protest against prevailing laxity, are sure to be the victims of persecution. And if their remonstrances cannot be silenced in any other way, there will not be lacking those who will suborn witnesses to sustain any accusation that may be plausibly brought against them. Especially is this true if, in their zeal for the truth, they may have been betrayed into any indiscretion of word or act.

It is sometimes the case that one becomes the victim of JEALOUSY AND ENVY. His talents, the influence he has with his brethren, the attention he attracts from the public, and his success in his enterprises, arouse the base passions of envy and jealousy in little minds of large pretensions and slender merit. The homage rendered to the one is by the other considered as so much tribute unjustly withheld from himself; and the success of the former, blighting the prospects of his competitor for pre-eminence, is considered by him a mortal offence. For this, all unconsciously to himself, the successful man is held personally responsible. Jealousy and envy first ripen into hatred, and hatred gives birth to conspiracy and intrigue. The shadow cast upon the interests of the jealous man can be removed only by leveling in the dust the object that intervenes between him and the light.

Thus, all unconsciously to himself, one may have an enemy to watch him, to garble his sayings, to pervert his actions, and to weave around him meshes that he may find it hard to break. Thus, as has been said, it is not impossible for one deserving the love and confidence of his brethren to find himself, through misapprehension, malice, or jealousy, an object of distrust, and arraigned before the Church for crimes his soul abhors. To such an one, excepting his consciousness of innocence, the only consolation is, that the Lord reigns. When such a lot as this befalls a pious man, what are his feelings and deportment?

1. He submits himself to the divine will, and patiently accepts the position assigned him. He acknowledges the providence of God in all things; and, though he knows he is the victim of misconception or of wickedness, he accepts it as the divine will that he should be placed in these trying circumstances. He may, and doubtless does, find it difficult to realize that he is arraigned under grave charges before his brethren; but he takes consolation in knowing that God has some wise purpose to accomplish in him or by him, and that He will make the wrath of man praise Him, and the remainder of wrath will restrain. You will not find him chafing under his condition; but with strong faith he lays hold of the promise that no temptation shall befall him except such as he shall be able to bear; and he even rejoices if it should be the Lord's will that he should suffer shame for His name. Like his fellow-servant Paul, he takes consolation in knowing that his bonds will somehow or other tend to the furtherance of the gospel. To the Lord's will he bows with humble submission; and he meekly takes the place of an accused man assigned him by His providence.

2. He will in all proper ways defend himself

against the charges alleged against him. This he owes not only to himself, but to his Master, whose truth is suffering in his person, and who designs that His cause shall be promoted by his good name. But,—

3. He will be careful to refrain from an indulgence of the spirit of his persecutors, and from a resort to the means employed by them. Is he reviled? He reviles not again. He has no grievous words to utter that stir up anger; but he prays for them that despitefully use and persecute him. Enormous as is the sin of his enemies, like the first Christian martyr, he prays that the Lord might not lay it to their charge. Is he the victim of misapprehension, or do circumstances seem to fasten guilt upon him? He recognizes the right and duty of his brethren to prosecute the investigation they have commenced. Nay, he encourages them to proceed, because in this way alone can he be relieved, and because he prefers to be unjustly condemned rather than that the sin which seems to attach to him should go unrebuked. Placing the best construction upon the course of his brethren of the Church, he labors candidly to remove their misapprehensions, or to unravel the meshes which circumstances have woven around him. His traducers, perhaps, have made appeals to prejudice to prepare the public mind for the favorable reception of the charge. Shall he meet them on their own ground, considering that the end justifies the

means? As soon as he receives intimation of their intentions, shall he make an appeal to the public through the newspapers, or by advertisements set up in conspicuous places, or by letters missive to all the neighboring churches, to be read in open conference? Shall he thus in advance assail the motives of these men, wicked though they be? Shall he inform the world that a conspiracy is formed against him for his destruction, and that the Church is under the control of the conspirators,—the willing instrument for the accomplishment of their nefarious designs? Shall he make an appeal to the sympathy of the public and of his brethren in the churches around, on the plea that he is to be made a victim on account of his piety or his faithfulness to sentiments they hold dear? His enemies, as he thinks, through prejudice, have in advance arrayed the Church against him. Shall he, to meet them by a like appeal to prejudice and public sympathy, attempt to array an outside influence of church-members and men of the world to OVERAWE the Church? Shall he form a party of outsiders to clamor in advance against the threatened arraignment, to attend at the trial, and, with lowering looks and disorderly utterances, to stand around him as his "friends," and, if the worst should happen, and he be expelled, to unite, with him at their head, in a combined assault upon the Church, with the intention to annihilate it, and, after accomplishing, as they suppose, their purposes, to march off with flying colors, proclaiming that not he, but the Church, has been excommunicated, and that he is the most proper church-member of them all? These are actions that are to be expected, not from a pious but a wicked man, who has no defence to make for his crimes, or who desires to organize for himself a sect that can sustain him in his wickedness and give him a victory over his hated rivals, or who can impart to him factitious greatness, influence, or pecuniary gain.

4. An innocent man arraigned is anxious that God's cause and Christ's Church should suffer as little as possible, preferring to be immolated himself rather than that principles dear to his heart should be subverted. He values his reputation as dearer than life; but he is not willing that this should be vindicated at the sacrifice of the principles and the forms that Christ has prescribed to be operative in such cases. He desires earnestly to be acquitted, and to retain his place among God's people; but even this high boon he will not accept at the price of the establishment of such principles in the churches of Christ as will make it impossible to discipline designing and wicked men. Far better, in his estimation, that he should be unjustly excommunicated, than that the churches should in effect give up the power to withdraw fellowship from all offenders, excepting from the weak and helpless. Never will he seek to obtain release on the ground that the

Church has not the power of putting away from Christ's professing people the wicked man who may be artful and influential. A pious man who is unjustly accused desires to be justified before the Church and the world; but he uses only the forms and appeals only to the principles that Christ has instituted, and which have been sanctioned by immemorial usage. He acknowledges the jurisdiction of the Church over him, and will accept of no justification before the world in terms, excepting that which he can obtain through the Church. And if, after all his lawful efforts to relieve himself, he should be finally condemned, he meekly submits to the Lord's will of purpose, knowing that He who has promised that all things shall work together for his good has some wise purpose to accomplish in him or by him. Suppose his enemies do glory over him, or the thoughtless point the finger of scorn at him: better these, infinitely, than triumph and notoriety and emolument at the expense of truth and a clear conscience. God not unfrequently permits his servants to pass through the fiery furnace, not only that the dross may be consumed, but that the pure GOLD MAY APPEAR. "By their fruits ye shall know them."

CHAPTER V.

WHAT IS "THE CHURCH" TO WHICH THE NEW TESTAMENT GIVES JURISDICTION OVER OFFENCES?

THE evangelists record but two instances in which the Saviour used the word "church." In each of these instances He employed it in a different sense. In Matt. xvi. 18, referring to the confession of Peter, He says, "Upon this rock I will build my church, and the gates of hell shall not prevail against it;" and in Matt. xviii. 17, "Tell it to the church," &c. The most casual glance will show that He could not have had in view the same object each time. The inspired penmen of the New Testament make the same distinction in its use. A careful collation of the passages in which the word is found will show that, in its relation to the kingdom of Christ, it has two meanings.

1. It is used to express the whole company of those who are saved by Him,—from righteous Abel down to the last one who shall be redeemed by His precious blood. The following passages may be cited to sustain this meaning: "Gave him to be head over all things to the church." Eph. i. 22. "Unto him be

glory in the church by Jesus Christ throughout all ages, world without end." Eph. iii. 21. (Here, this glory is to Him in the church in heaven, world without end,—long after all local churches shall cease to exist.) "To the intent that now unto the principalities and powers in heavenly places might be known by the church the manifold wisdom of God." Eph. iii. 10. "The husband is the head of the wife, even as Christ is the head of the Church." Eph. v. 23, &c. "But ye have come unto Mount Zion, and unto the city of the living God, the heavenly Jerusalem, and to an innumerable company of angels, and to the general assembly and church of the first-born which are written in heaven." Heb. xii. 22. Other passages of a like nature may be quoted; but let these suffice.

The Greek word *ecclesia*, which is translated "church," signifies an assembly. It is objected that it cannot with propriety be applied to the whole company of believers, since they never have met in an assembly on earth. The last passage quoted, however, meets this objection, by suggesting that the place of assembling is not earth, but heaven.

The constituents of this assembly are those who have been called by God's grace, regenerated by God's Spirit, and redeemed by Christ's blood. From the time of Abel they have been gathering together to the place of meeting. In all time, and from all regions, they have been converging to the heavenly Jerusalem; and when the last of the redeemed shall be prepared to answer to his name, they will constitute in fact what they always have in God's purpose, the general assembly and church universal of Christ gathered together in heaven.

This cannot be the body to whom the Saviour has given jurisdiction over offences. It possesses no visibility excepting in the persons of the individual members of it who so live as to show the power of Divine grace; it contains no external organization or officers; and it never will meet together in time. It is maintained by some that the church universal is composed of the aggregate of Baptist churches,—that the Baptist denomination and the church universal are synonymous terms. To this opinion there are the following difficulties:

1st. This would be to include in the general assembly and church of the first-born which are written in heaven, some who have never been converted, and who will finally perish. Every one will grant that many, if not all, the Baptist churches, may contain persons who will live in hypocrisy or self-delusion, and die in impenitence and go to perdition.

2d. This would be to exclude from the general assembly and church of the first-born many who have been converted and saved in heaven. On this principle, all the Old Testament worthies would be excluded from the universal church; though we are told that Abraham and Isaac and Jacob, and all the prophets, shall sit down in the kingdom of heaven.

These and multitudes of others now in glory died before the formation of the first Baptist church in Jerusalem. On this principle, the thief on the cross will be excluded, though the Saviour said to him, "This day shalt thou be with me in paradise;" and even John the Baptist, the Forerunner of Christ, would be shut out; since he never was baptized and never was a member of a Baptist church.

If Christ was made head over all things only to the aggregate of Baptist churches, then He does not and never did bear that relation to Abraham and a vast multitude of others, though they were redeemed by His precious blood.

3d. This would be to use the term "church" in the sense in which we deny it to the Romish hierarchy and other organizations of vast territorial extent.

The Baptist denomination, since the dispersion of the disciples in Jerusalem, never did and never will meet together in one assembly on earth. If, then, the Baptist denomination in the world, which cannot meet together in one assembly, can be called a church, how can we deny to the Methodist Episcopal organization, or the Presbyterian organization, the name of church, on the plea that they cannot thus meet together? The Baptist (and we think the scriptural) local organization is called a church, because it constitutes an assembly capable of meeting together in one place. Upon what principles, then, can we call the Baptist denomination a church, when it is composed of distinct churches, that by the very theory of their organization must remain distinct, and which will lose their distinctive characteristics and become annihilated when they are merged into one general organization? If they are merged together in fact, they are annihilated in fact; if the merging is a mere mental conception, then the mental conception is an annihilation of the true scriptural conception. According to the signification of the word ECCLESIA, it is as easy to conceive of the church or assembly of all the Romanists in the world as of the church or assembly of all the Baptist churches in the world. Nay, easier, since in their case nothing prevents but the physical impossibility, while in the case of the Baptist churches to this physical impossibility are added the thousands and thousands of barriers afforded by the organization of each. An assembly composed of individuals, however impossible, may be conceived; but what imagination can picture an assembly whose components are local churches? But

4th. If it is correct in any sense to call the aggregate of Baptist churches A church, where and what is the general organization? A number of machines placed in contact side by side do not become one vast machine: so the array of thousands and thousands of Baptist churches do not in fact or mental conception constitute one general church. They still remain what they were before,—the churches of the Lord Jesus Christ. Here are organizations; but where is

THE organization par excellence? Where is the head of this church, either in the form of Pope, or Bishop, or Pastor—where its place of meeting and what its functions?—Let the constituents of the church universal be regenerated persons, the place of meeting heaven, and the period when they shall completely assemble, the time when all Christ's redeemed people shall be gathered together in one, and we can perceive the propriety of the term applied to it,—"the general assembly and church of the first-born whose names are written in heaven." Then can we see the pertinence and truth of the apostle's declaration when he says, "Christ also loved the church and gave himself for it;—that he might present it to himself *a glorious church, not having spot, or wrinkle, or any such thing; but that it should be holy and without blemish.*" Eph. v. 25–27. Christ's church universal is composed exclusively of regenerated persons from all Christian organizations, and from no organizations, who have no external bond of union, and who will never all meet together until they constitute the general assembly above.

But this cannot be the church to whom Christ gives the jurisdiction of offences.

2. The word "church" is used again in the New Testament to designate a local society, composed of those, and those only, who profess regeneration and faith in Christ, and who have been immersed upon a profession of that faith,—who are able to meet

together in one place, and who observe the ordinances and maintain the worship of God. This is the only external organization which the New Testament designates by the term "Church." To these local churches the followers of Christ unite themselves, securing first their fellowship by convincing them that they have believed with the heart unto righteousness, and submitting to the ordinance of baptism, which is an indispensable prerequisite to membership. These bodies in the management of their internal affairs Christ makes *independent* of each other and of all the world besides; and to these he delegates *sovereignty* over their members, enjoining them to watch over them in love, to instruct them in the truth as it is in Jesus, to comfort the feeble-minded, to warn the unruly, to restore the wandering, and, if need be, to put away from among themselves wicked persons. It is the *Local Church*, then, to which Christ has given jurisdiction over offences.

CHAPTER VI.

THE RELATION THE PASTOR SUSTAINS TO CORRECTIVE DISCIPLINE.

WHAT relation does the pastor of the church bear to corrective discipline?—and what are his duties in the premises? There is no question more important than this. Often have difficulties been aggravated, and churches torn to pieces, because pastors did not have a clear conception of the relations they sustain to cases of discipline. The question at the head of this paragraph will be answered, 1st, Upon the supposition that the pastor is, himself, involved in the difficulty; and, 2d, Upon the supposition that he is free from entanglement.

1. Should the pastor be involved as one of the parties at variance, or be charged with a public offence, what should be the course of proceeding?

Ans.—Precisely that which is prescribed in the case of a private member of the church. He should lay aside his authority as presiding officer, and take his seat among his brethren; for surely no man would assert the claim to preside in his own case. If he has a private grievance against one of his brethren, he is to pursue the "gospel steps" prescribed to others; and if, in the last resort, he tells his grievance to the Church, he is to stand aside, and permit the Church to appoint, temporarily, an officer in his place. If he is charged with a "public offence," he is to be dealt with like a private member, with the single exception that an accusation is not to be *received* against him except from the mouth of two or three witnesses. The question whether a minister can be dealt with and expelled without the intervention of a Council or Presbytery will be discussed in a succeeding number.

2. Upon the supposition that the pastor is himself free from entanglement, what relation does he sustain to corrective discipline? This question will be answered, 1st, In relation to cases of "private" dealing; and, 2d, In relation to cases of "public" dealing.

1st. What is the pastor's duty in regard to cases of variance between brethren? To this it is answered,—

(1.) To instil into his members in advance, by his ministry, such principles as to *prevent* variances; and, after their occurrence, to enlighten them with such instructions from the Scriptures as to show them how to manage them according to the mind of Christ. Ministers of the gospel should see to it, that their members, young as well as old, are thoroughly instructed in regard to scriptural polity; and that in this they are perfect, thoroughly furnished unto all good works.

(2.) It is his duty to see that every case of "private" dealing, if brought into the Church at all, be introduced according to the Saviour's directions.

(3.) It is his duty to maintain the strictest neutrality as between the parties. *Questions of order* he is to decide: *principles* which are applicable to the case, he should announce in conference, and in the pulpit, with boldness and plainness. But as soon as he begins to decide upon questions of fact, or to announce as to who, in his opinion, is guilty or who innocent, he trenches upon the prerogative of the Church, which alone has the right to decide upon such points. He should keep profoundly locked in his breast his opinions of the facts, and of the guilt or innocence of the contestants. Just so soon as he indicates an opinion, he ceases to be an umpire between those at variance, and the moderator of the Church, and descends to be the head of one of the parties which may be formed or forming in the Church. The pastoral relation, with ministers who violate this principle, can never survive more than one serious church-difficulty.

(4.) *When all believe that he is in fact a neutral as between the contending brethren*, the pastor has it in his power to bring the pulpit to bear with telling effect upon the adjustment of the difficulty. And this he should not fail to do. In serious difficulties, he should direct his attention to the accomplishment of two objects: *First*, to prevent the formation of two parties in the Church, with the members at variance at the head of each respectively; and, *second*, to make the combatants themselves ashamed and tired of their relations. In every case of variance of long standing, where both parties are wrong in feeling and equally matched in strength, the attempt of each inevitably will be to array to himself in advance as many partisans in the Church as possible. This the pastor in the pulpit can prevent. It should be his purpose to isolate the case,—to fence the contestants off to themselves, and, if they must fight, to make them fight it out alone. To accomplish this, he should never in the pulpit refer directly to the case. This would be very *malapropos*. The Scriptures abound in principles which he can so discuss as to make the pious members of the Church afraid to involve themselves, or by their act to encourage either of the parties in his course. The particular case should never be mentioned; but the remarks should be so directed as to graze along by it, and suggest it to the mind of the hearer. When the members of the church have been thoroughly drilled into neutrality and silence, then the case becomes more simple; and the pastor can bring all the artillery of the pulpit to bear upon the individuals at variance. To these we should give no rest, and afford no consolation. They should not be permitted ever to retire from the sanctuary without being wounded and bleeding. They should be made to feel that the gospel has nothing for them but condemnation. To accomplish this, no little address is necessary. The pastor should never in the pulpit refer to the case in terms. This would be a personality and offensive. But the contending brethren should be compelled to believe that, somehow or other, he is preaching to nobody but to them; and yet they must find nothing in his remarks to complain of him about. What he says must be in the form of principles equally applicable to both in common, so that the blow leveled may not be weakened by the suspicion that he is discriminating for or against either. In this way, *if they are thoroughly convinced that the pastor has not taken sides in the issue between them,* and they are Christians, it will not be long before they become heartily sick of the position they occupy, and ready to hail with pleasure a proposition of some mutual friend to mediate between them. In the management of cases of this kind, time, prudence, and faithfulness are all-important.

2. What relation does the pastor sustain to cases of "public" dealing? The same principles that are to govern him in private dealing hold good here. The reader may make the application for himself. It will be enough to say that *it is never his duty to arraign one before the Church,* or to charge him in private with any offence he has not confessed, unless he (the pastor) witnessed the commission of the act. In the pulpit and the chair, the pastor bears, in many

respects, the same relation to the Church in the trial of public offenders, that the judge upon the bench does to the court in the trial of criminals. It is the duty and prerogative of others to arraign the offender, to array the testimony, and to prosecute to conviction. To the pastor it is reserved to see that the trial is commenced and prosecuted upon gospel principles. From the beginning to the end, he is to intimate no opinion, publicly or privately, of the guilt or innocence of the accused who pleads not guilty; but to hold the scales of justice even. The Saviour has devolved upon His *Churches*, and not upon His ministers, the responsibility and the duty of condemning and putting away from them wicked persons. If, however, the Church permits immoralities to be perpetrated by its members with impunity, it is the prerogative and the duty of the pastor—avoiding personalities—to give a scriptural delineation of the crimes committed; to hold them up to public reprobation; and to give the Church no rest until it is willing to do its duty. And all this, too, without saying in terms that the crime has been committed by any of his members, or tolerated by his Church.

In answer, then, to the question, What relation does the pastor sustain to a case of discipline? it is said,

1. He has entire control of all the *principles* that are operative in the case; and he should announce them on all proper occasions from the pulpit and the chair.

2. He has nothing to do with the *facts*, or with the guilt or innocence of parties; and he should keep profoundly silent on these, giving no one occasion to infer what his opinions are. By this means,—

1st. He will be an umpire between the parties— and he can gain unobstructed access to them for the gospel principles with which he would influence their judgments and their consciences.

2d. He will retain an influence with all which he can wield for the good of the church in the progress of the trial.

3d. He will avoid the formation of a faction against him, which may embitter his existence, cripple his influence, and terminate in the severance of the pastoral relation.

CHAPTER VII.

DEDUCTIONS FROM PREVIOUS PRINCIPLES—CHURCH SOVEREIGNTY AND INDEPENDENCE.

DEDUCTION 1.—*Local churches have exclusive jurisdiction over their members.* This proposition asserts two things:—*first*, a local church has jurisdiction over its members; and second, this jurisdiction belongs to it exclusively. But they can both be proved by the same process. Here there is no room for abstract reasoning. The only proof admissible is that derived from the New Testament. To the New Testament alone, then, let the appeal be made. To the churches belong exclusive jurisdiction over their members, because,—

1. The Saviour *gave* them such jurisdiction. This is clearly implied in His directions to the offended brother, "Tell it unto the church; but if he neglect to hear the church, let him be to thee as an heathen man and a publican." Matt. xviii. 17.

2. Paul *acknowledges* this jurisdiction when he exhorts the Corinthians to discipline the incestuous man. "Do not ye judge them that are within? [*i.e.* your own members.] Therefore put away from

among yourselves that wicked person." 1 Cor. v. 12, 13.

3. In the Revelations the Saviour *commends* one church for exercising it. To the church at Ephesus He commands John to write, "I know thy works, and thy labor, and thy patience, and how thou canst not bear them which are evil; and thou hast tried them which say they are apostles, and are not, and hast found them liars. But this thou hast, that thou hatest the deeds of the Nicolaitanes, which I also hate." Rev. ii. 2–6.

4. He *condemns* other churches for not exercising it, and enforcing discipline. To the church at Pergamos He says, "But I have a few things against thee, because thou hast there them that hold the doctrine of Balaam, who taught Balak to cast a stumbling-block before the children of Israel, to eat things sacrificed unto idols, and to commit fornication. So hast thou also them that hold the doctrine of the Nicolaitanes, which thing I hate. Repent, or else I will come to thee quickly," &c. Rev. ii. 14, 15, 16. To the church at Thyatira He says, "Notwithstanding, I have a few things against thee, because thou sufferest that woman Jezebel, which calleth herself a prophetess, to teach and to seduce my servants to commit fornication, and to eat things sacrificed to idols." Rev. ii. 20.

Now, jurisdiction implies supremacy and power. If "that woman Jezebel" could have refused to be tried, or in other ways to acknowledge the jurisdiction of the Church over her, then the church at Thyatira could have pleaded that it lacked the power to call her to account; or if others, either churches, church officers, or committees, had joint jurisdiction, the Church might have shifted the responsibility, and pleaded that she had been disabled by the opposition or indifference of others. No. It was the duty of the Church to restrain, or to put away from the professed followers of Christ, wicked persons; and the Church was vested with the power to do so. Hence the condemnation passed by the Saviour *upon her and her alone.* Under Christ, every local church has supreme jurisdiction over its members. It can, without permission asked of an offender, or of any other individuals or organizations in the world, arraign him, try him, condemn him, and, if need be, expel him. This jurisdiction is commonly expressed by the term *sovereignty*. Against the use of this term, of late, strenuous objection has been urged. This objection may be leveled either against the appositeness of the term to convey the idea, or else against the idea itself designed to be conveyed by it.

First.—Why is not the term an appropriate one? It is answered, "It is absurd to call that a *sovereign* body which is *subject* in all things. Christ is the only King in Zion, and, therefore, the only sovereign." This objection is urged by those who grant and maintain that every church is *independent*. The so-called independence of the churches, and the consequences drawn from it, constitute the main ground of their arguments against church sovereignty. Now, upon the same principles upon which they repudiate sovereignty, how easy will it be to show that there can be no such thing as independence. If the Church cannot be sovereign because it is subject to Christ, then it cannot be independent, either, because it is DEpendent upon Christ in all things. So, you see, it is as broad as it is long; and if there is no sovereignty, then there is no independence either. Upon the principle of the objection, there is not now, and never has been, *a sovereign State* in the world; for God reigns supreme, the only absolute sovereign in the universe. In relation to God, all nations are subject and dependent; but in relation to their subjects and to one another they are sovereign and independent. So gospel churches, in relation to Christ, are both subject and dependent in all things; but in relation to their own members and to one another they are both sovereign and independent. So it will be seen that not absolute and inherent, but *delegated, sovereignty*, is claimed for gospel churches. And all that is meant is, that under the law of Christ, in the enforcement of discipline, they have supreme jurisdiction over their disorderly members.

Second.—But it may be that the objection is

leveled at the idea legitimately conveyed by the term "sovereign." Will any one maintain that a church has no right to arraign, try, and expel an offender, that in these things her members are not *subject* to her? Will any one maintain that it is optional with the member whether or not he will submit to a trial, when arraigned on charges before his church, and that a church, when endeavoring to put away from her number a wicked person, cannot succeed, unless she obtain his consent, and the consent of those that are without? If so, then is there no such thing as *corrective church discipline*. Members may withdraw from the church, but there can be no such thing as withdrawing fellowship from them; and excommunication will mean nothing more than that the disorderly member has given his consent to relieve the church from any further responsibility for him. If churches have not the POWER to deal with and excommunicate disorderly persons without their consent, then, when the Saviour instructed the offended to carry the offender before the church, He but MOCKED HIM; when He praised the church at Ephesus for trying the false apostles, He gave them credit for that which was but TEMERITY and PRESUMPTION; and when He chided Pergamos and Thyatira for tolerating wicked persons, *He unjustly held them accountable for that over which they had no control.* It was their misfortune, and not their fault, that these disorderly persons were retained; since, according to the supposition, they had not the *power* to put them away. Surely, on reflection, it must be granted that, under Christ, every local church, in enforcing discipline, has supreme control of its offending members—that, in administering the laws of Christ, it has the *power* to discipline its members without asking the consent of them or of anybody else.

Sovereignty and independence are not synonymous terms. In an earthly kingdom, *sovereign*, as a term, is the correlative of *subject*, and implies the power to *govern*, either under law or without it, as the sovereign may be limited or absolute in power. *Independence* in a State marks its relations not to its own people, but *to other States*, and signifies *freedom from control by other States*. So church sovereignty marks the relation the church bears, not to other churches, but to its own members, and signifies *her power to govern them*, under the laws of Christ. Church independence marks the relation that the church sustains, not to her members, but to other churches, and signifies *her freedom from their control*. The *sovereignty* of a church is subverted, when her members successfully rebel against her authority; as when a member under charges refuses to be tried, and successfully tears himself free from her jurisdiction. The *independence* of a church is infringed upon when other churches, associations, or councils, either voluntarily, or at the instigation of her recusant member, interfere with her discipline, or otherwise attempt forcibly to control her. Under Christ, a local church is both sovereign and independent. It is not claimed, however, that she has the power to make laws. It is granted and maintained that Christ is the only lawgiver, and that all that is left for the Church to do, in the case of offences, is to administer and execute the law. It has no legislative power; but Christ has invested it with *judicial and executive powers.*

First.—The Church is invested by Christ with the power to arraign and try its members.

Question 1.—"**But may not a member refuse to be tried?**"

Ans.—He may SAY he refuses; and so may a citizen under the jurisdiction of one of our courts say he will not heed a citation. But what will be the result? If the suit be a civil one, and he refuses to appear, either in person or by attorney, it goes against him by default; if it be a criminal one, then one of two things will inevitably happen: either he will fall into the hands of the power he endeavors to elude, and be tried anyhow, or he becomes a fugitive from his country. A church-member in disorder may say he refuses to be tried; but if the church be true to Christ, to herself, and to the culprit, he will be tried notwithstanding.

Question 2.—"**Suppose he does actually refuse to be tried: what then?**"

Ans.—He only adds to his other sins those of contumacy and rebellion. "He neglects to hear the church" in its citations; and if he were innocent in all things else, persisting in this attitude, she is bound to make him bear the relation to her of "an heathen man and a publican." There is not a church in Christendom that would not feel itself in duty bound to expel one maintaining this attitude, whatever may be his characteristics in other respects.

Question 3.—"But suppose the arraigned differs from the Church in regard to the kind of offence and the method of proceeding?"

Ans.—The church is the only judge of the law and the fact; and her decision is final. Either the church or the arraigned is to decide all questions raised. If the arraigned, then no guilty person could be punished; for he would always quash proceedings on some plea. In the language of Bro. J. S. Baker, in another connection, "Satan and his subjects are ever fruitful in inventions. An offender, therefore, will seldom want for a plausible objection to every rule of discipline that is applicable to his case, even though such be expressly given in Scripture." (p. 270.) In a previous number, it was shown that, in no event could injustice be done to an innocent man, if the church rule his offence to be "public," when he thinks it to be strictly "private." But it may be asked, "Is not something due the cause of Christ from an innocent man accused? and does he escape responsibility and sin, if he permits the church to go on in violation of the law of Christ?" To this it is answered, that if he raises the point of order, and the church overrule him, not he, but the church, is responsible. Whatever sin there may be in the sight of God and man, he is free from it. But, besides, what else can he do to stay proceedings, without himself committing a greater sin than that he so conscientiously protests against? Shall he conscientiously attempt to arrest proceedings by rebelling against the authority Christ has committed to His Church, and refusing to be tried any further? Strange conscientiousness that, which attempts to prevent another from committing a sin by perpetrating a greater sin itself! And, besides, conscientiousness in this connection can with difficulty be distinguished from an attempt to evade justice. This is precisely the course a wicked man would pursue,—one who is fighting for victory, or to thwart an adversary in the church,—if he dared to do so, and was convinced that he had a sufficient number outside of the church to sustain him. A man does not show his conscientiousness by acting on the principle, "Let us do evil that good may come."

Question 4.—"But does not a church that rejects the law of Christ as laid down in Matt. xviii. cease to be a church of Christ, and is not the member released from all obligations to it?"

Ans.—Please stick to the original proposition. The case before us is this:—On a point raised by the arraigned, *the church thinks* the offence comes under

1 Cor. v., while *he thinks* it comes under Matt. xviii. Here the church rejects not the law, *but the offender's interpretation of it.* The most that can be said, then, is that the church has wilfully or inadvertently misapplied the law. The latter will always, in a judgment of charity, be ascribed to her. In "mixed offences," (see Chap. I. of this series,) where the act is a crime against religion and morality, and the object of it a brother, it is always easy for an offender who is a designing man, or whose head is confused, to mystify the minds of others by raising a point of this kind. Bear in mind, however, that, according to the supposition, the church does not avowedly reject the law of Christ, but only commits an error in its application. If, then, the objection contained in your question has any force, see to what it brings us. See what is the general principle that must be deduced for the offender to stand on and be sustained in his rebellion against the church. It is this:—*Whenever a church commits an error, it becomes annihilated.* On this principle, there is no church now in the world; for all have, during their existence, made mistakes and committed errors. We are happy, however, to know from the Scriptures that such an effect does not follow from such a cause, and that the world is not in this sad and irretrievable condition. The church at Corinth for a long time permitted an incestuous man to remain quiet and undisturbed in her communion; and division and

party spirit raged within her borders. Some were for Paul, and some for Apollos, and some for Cephas, and some for Christ. Here were grave errors, serious omissions of duty, and reprehensible sins. Was the church at Corinth annihilated? Paul did not seem to think so. And we nowhere read that the incestuous man, when arraigned, raised this point, and barred off the infliction of the penalty due to his crimes by declaring the church annihilated. Against the majority of "the seven churches which are in Asia," Christ brings serious accusations. To one He says, "I have somewhat against thee, because thou hast left thy first love;" two others He chides because they retain among themselves disorderly and wicked persons; to another He says, "I have not found thy works perfect before God." "I know thy works, that thou hast a name that thou livest, and art dead;" and to another still He brings the charge of lukewarmness, threatening to spew it out of His mouth. Yet His apostle, in addressing these very things to them, styles them "the seven churches which are in Asia." It cannot be true, then, that when a church commits an error in the application of the law in Matt. xviii., or in any other way, it becomes annihilated.

But suppose we grant, for the sake of the argument, that the commission of an error by her will annihilate the church: then the question comes up, who is to decide that an error has been committed, and that the church has been annihilated? The arraigned man? If so, what designing and wicked persons can be tried? How easy will it be for an unscrupulous man to join issue with the church on some point he may raise, whether pertinently or not, and thus annihilate the church and ward off from himself the retribution due to his crimes! How many criminals arraigned before our courts of justice would be condemned, if it was the prerogative of the prisoner at the bar to decide all the points of law raised by his counsel, with whom he is in collusion? Nay, more: what prospect would there be of enforcing the criminal laws of the country, if the prisoner at the bar had the power to disband and annihilate the court whenever IT differed from him in the interpretation of law? Whenever one arraigned before a church makes such a plea as this, it proves nothing more than that he has no better plea to urge.

On the subject of the right and duty of a church, when even a purely "private" case has been informally brought before it, Bro. Joseph S. Baker speaks conclusively and forcibly as follows:—

"A. charges B. with trespasses committed against himself, before he pursues the course prescribed by the Saviour. B., in return, charges A. with a violation of the rule to which we have referred, and pleads, perhaps, that the church has no right to deal with him, as the case was informally brought before it. Such a plea is evidently invalid. The truth is, they are both offenders, and the church is bound to investigate and to act on the cases of both. But, as she cannot act on both simultaneously, the question may arise, which case should be first taken up? We answer, unhesitatingly, the case of B.; and that for two reasons: 1st. Because the offence of B. was committed prior to that of A., and was first brought to the notice of the church. 2d. Because A's. offence grew out of that of B. Properly, therefore, to adjudicate the case of A., we must acquaint ourselves with those circumstances in the conduct of B. which tended to aggravate or palliate the offence of the former. But to do this it would be necessary to enter fully into the investigation of the conduct of B. The case is as clear as the sun in a cloudless sky at noonday.

"We have frequently known churches to dismiss cases indefinitely, because there was some irregularity in the manner in which they were brought before them. These generally prove, too, FINAL dismissions. If we are right in the views expressed in the preceding part of this article, that church is wrong which pursues either of these courses. 'He that knoweth to do good and doeth it not, to him it is sin.' By parity of reasoning, that church which knows of the existence of an evil in it, and neglects to correct it promptly, must be viewed as guilty before God.

"When an individual is charged with criminal conduct, if, instead of replying to the charges brought against him, he endeavors to criminate others, he affords strong presumptive evidence of his own guilt. He acts upon the same principle with the thief, who, when the officer of justice and the mob are at his heels, raises the cry, and cries loudest of all, 'Stop thief! stop thief!' His principle is to evade justice by diverting attention from himself to some other individual. To prevent your plucking the beam out of his own eye, he would set you to picking at the mote in his brother's eye."—*Periodical Library*, Vol. 1, No. IV. (1847), pp. 264, 265.

It must be granted that the church possesses judicial power,—that it has the right to arraign and try its disorderly members.

In the last number it was shown that the Church, in the exercise of delegated sovereignty, has the right to arraign and try its disorderly members; and that such members can in no way escape her jurisdiction. To what was said there, it might be added, If the Church has not such jurisdiction as will enable it to arraign and try its disorderly members, then one of two things must be inevitably true: either the disorderly members are irresponsible and can be arraigned by nobody, or else they are subject to a jurisdiction outside of the Church. If the former be true, then the Scriptures authorize no corrective discipline, and there is no remedy for disorder and crime. If the latter be true, then to whom does such jurisdiction belong? To preachers and committees? Then should brethren cease their denunciations of Methodist circuit-riders and their committees for exercising this very prerogative. Does this jurisdiction belong to other churches, to associations, or to councils, whether directly or by appeal? Then are we Presbyterians in fact, if not in name. Surely it must be granted that local churches have the power to arraign and try their disorderly members. Now, if in these things disorderly members are *subject* to their churches, in these things have their churches the *sovereignty* over them. It remains to be shown in this connection—

2. That the Church has *executive authority*. She can expel all whom she tries and condemns. "Therefore, put away from among yourselves that wicked person." 1 Cor. v. 13.

Question 1.—"But can a church expel by majority?"

Ans.—It is always desirable that in a matter of such serious import as the expulsion of one from the privileges of the fold of Christ, there should be unanimity. In some of our churches, therefore, there is a rule requiring that in all matters touching fellowship the vote shall be unanimous. And the custom is to inquire of the minority whether they will acquiesce in the decision of the majority. If they consent to submit, and thus promise not to make this difference of opinion the ground of alienation and confusion, the inquiry proceeds no further, and the decision of the majority is recorded. But if the minority refuse to acquiesce, then the custom is to labor with them to bring them to right feelings and right views. This effort is to be made with patience and perseverance. It may be that the majority may become convinced that the opposition is well founded, and that they may be induced to stay proceedings, and to reconsider their action. But if it be manifested that the opposition is factious, then it is customary to *require* the minority to submit, and, if they refuse to obey, to treat them as public offenders, and, if necessary, to expel them. While the design of all this is to produce, if possible, harmony and unanimity, it is, at the same time, an assertion of the *right of the majority to rule, and the duty of the minority to submit.*

The assertion implied in the question at the beginning of the above paragraph is, *No one can be expelled excepting by a unanimous vote;* i.e. if any member objects. If this proposition be true, then if the woman whom the incestuous man at Corinth was claiming as his wife had been a member of the church, or if any other man in the church had been guilty of the same crime, he could not have been "put away." If but one should vote no, to the proposition to expel, the vote would not be unanimous. Then two wicked and abandoned men may mutually retain each other in the church, though one thousand should vote to put them away. Can a principle be correct which involves such consequences as these? Bro. Baker, in reasoning against the absurd proposition that the minority can "demand the exclusion of an individual whom the majority believe to be innocent," incidentally, but conclusively, answers the question above. After showing from the Scriptures that the decisions of the Church were ordinarily made by the lifting up of the hands of its members, he observes, "Now, we cannot account for this voting, by the lifting up of the hands, if it was not to ascertain the will of the *majority*. But we are not left to infer from *general* principles the course pursued by the primitive Church in the exclusion of members. We have the *express* testimony of an inspired apostle that in at least one case of exclusion the individual was excluded not by the *few*, but by the *many*. 'Sufficient to such a man [one that had been excluded] is this punishment WHICH WAS INFLICTED OF MANY.' 2 Cor. ii. 6. The word here rendered 'many' is *pleionon*, which signifies the *greater part*,—the *majority*. On this subject, then, the Scripture is *explicit* and *conclusive:* NOTHING CAN BE MORE SO. That passage is sufficient, of itself, to show what was the practice of the Church in apostolic times."—*Per. Lib.* p. 324.

Question 2.—"But may a minority never pronounce a majority to be no longer a church of Christ, and declare themselves to be the true Church?"

This question is answered unhesitatingly in the affirmative. There are cases in which a minority may pronounce the majority no longer a Church. But please notice the discriminations that are made, and the grounds upon which alone the question is thus answered. Whenever the Church, not only in fact, but *ostensibly* and by *profession*, departs from the faith and order that Christ has given, it ceases to be a Baptist church. For instance: If it, *by act* and *by profession*, denies the parity of the ministry, and introduces episcopacy; if it denies that the immersion of a professed believer is alone baptism, and avows and practices infant sprinkling; if it rescinds its articles of faith, and substitutes for them avowedly the doctrines of Campbellism or any other heresy; if it should by resolution deny church sovereignty, *i.e.* its jurisdiction over its disorderly members; if it should deny church independence, and subject itself with other churches to a form of Presbyterianism, making appellate tribunals in a series rising from conferences through councils, associations, and General Associations, up to General Conventions; if she should by vote and record declare that drunkenness, lying, fornication, theft, libel, profanity, and other crimes that the Scriptures reprehend, are no crimes, and avowedly encourage her members to practice them; if by vote and record she decides to do these, or any one of them, a minority may pronounce themselves the true church, and the courts of the country would sustain them in their claim. But, you perceive, this is not the case before us. In my admission, the persons protesting and unchurching are not the parties arraigned, or otherwise personally involved, but those who, having nothing personally at stake, are standing up solely for the honor of the Master and the constitution of His Church. They are struggling not to keep off censure from themselves, but to prevent the Church from being metamorphosed into a synagogue of Satan, or into another form of Christian organization which they do not consider scriptural. But this has no pertinence to a case of discipline, where the charges are for such things as are recognized to be crimes by the Scriptures.

This is the question you ought to have asked:— "Can an arraigned man and his supporters, the minority, pronounce the majority no church, because of the manner in which they conduct his trial? and can they relieve him from expulsion by proclaiming themselves as alone the true Church?" To answer this question in the affirmative, and to practice on this principle, is to make it impossible to discipline a plausible and wicked man, and to rend a church into fragments every time it may attempt to enforce discipline upon a man of this kind. How easy would it be for such a one to plant himself upon some great scriptural principle, which he may arbitrarily insist is applicable to the case, and, if the church should deny its applicability, to go off accompanied by his relations, his personal friends, and his business associates! If he is adroit, he may even succeed in mystifying many honest and disinterested minds. But my objector wishes to bring me back to the admissions I have made in answer to his first question; and he wishes to inquire,—

"Are not the Saviour's directions for the government of private offences of vital importance? If, then, the majority of a church, in the management of a case of discipline, disregard those directions, cannot the minority (leaving the arraigned out of the question) stand up for the Saviour's rule, and unchurch the majority?" Let us see what you mean by "disregard." *First.* The Church may honestly *mistake* that for a public which is merely a private offence; or, *Second*, Knowing and acknowledging it to be a private offence, prematurely introduced, it may decide to entertain it anyhow. Let us see whether either of these is a "disregard" of the Saviour's directions, and whether they furnish sufficient grounds for the minority to unchurch the majority. If the majority honestly *mistake* the nature of the offence, it has only committed an error; and we have shown in the previous number that a church is not annihilated whenever it commits an error. For the same reasons, a mistake made by the church in reference to the nature of an offence does not furnish sufficient grounds for a minority to unchurch the majority. But, *second,* Suppose the majority, knowing and acknowledging that it is a private offence prematurely introduced, should nevertheless entertain it: what then? I answer, they may, like Bro. Baker, and other distinguished writers on church discipline, believe that these directions are addressed primarily to the offended, to guide *his* deportment, and that the church has the *right,* if it think best, to take into consideration the conduct of her offending member, even though the case may have been irregularly and, if you please, wickedly brought before her. In all this these writers may be mistaken; and the church, in acting on this principle, may commit an error without designing to "disregard" the instructions of Christ. Now, as has been shown already, an error unintentionally committed does not annihilate a church, nor does it afford ground sufficient for a minority to unchurch the majority. Infallibility does not reside in a church, either in its majority or in its minority. On a question whether a church can entertain a private offence prematurely and irregularly introduced, honest differences of opinion may be tolerated; and surely a mistake on the subject cannot involve annihilation. If a church were *by vote and record* to resolve that it would "disregard" or erase from the Revelation received by it the 18th of Matthew, or any other part of the Scriptures, great or small, it would resolve itself into an infidel fraternity, and the *believers* in its midst should repudiate and denounce it. But surely *the avowed rejection* of the 18th of Matthew, and *the erroneous application of its law,* while its binding force is acknowledged, are very different things.

So it will be seen that a member under dealing cannot escape expulsion by retiring with a minority of the church; and that such minority, so far from shielding him by their rebellion, subject themselves to the same penalty he endures. There is not a church in Christendom, true to the Master and to herself, that would not, in these circumstances, expel all her recusants. And if the revolters should afterwards, with or without organization, call themselves *the* church, or *a* church, whatever else they may be, they are not a Baptist church, which we consider to be synonymous with a gospel church. Whatever may be their pretensions or their claims, *they are excommunicated Baptists,* and should be so regarded and treated by all who reverence the authority of the King in Zion.

In conclusion, then, it must be granted that in the exercise of delegated sovereignty the Church has *executive authority.* She can expel all whom she tries and condemns.

Question 3.—"Can a church expel a *minister* without the intervention of a Council or Presbytery?"

The answer to this question must be reserved to the next chapter.

CHAPTER VIII.

CHURCH SOVEREIGNTY, CONTINUED—TRIAL OF MINISTERS.

Question 3.—"CAN a *minister* be tried and expelled without the intervention of a Presbytery or Council?"

Direct expressions in the Scriptures, as well as the general principles laid down therein, authorize us, in our opinion, to answer this question in the affirmative. Not a few distinguished and deservedly influential names, however, may be quoted against us. Baker, Crowell, Sands, the lamented Meredith, and others, all give a different answer, and fortify it by many plausible arguments. It becomes the present writer, then, to express himself with diffidence, and to proceed no further than he can plainly show that he is sustained by the Scriptures.

1. My first remark, then, is that no passage in the Bible, *in direct terms*, instructs the church to call in a Presbytery or Council when she would try a minister holding membership with her; nor is a single example given in the Scriptures where one was tried with such intervention. No one, it is pre-

sumed, will call this in question. If so, let the precept be quoted or the example cited. The church is told how she is to "receive an accusation against an elder;" but it is not hinted to her that she cannot proceed, in other respects, in his trial, in the same way in which she conducts the process against any other member accused. This of itself is significant. But,—

2. Paul *directs* the Galatians to excommunicate the false ministers who were teaching that it was necessary to be justified by the law. "I would they were even cut off which trouble you." v. 12. "And this they were to do in the exercise of their Christian liberty. v. 13." (Crowell.) To the church alone the address is directed; and no hint is given that it needed the help of a Council or Presbytery. But, it may be said, these were *false* teachers. True: it was not to be expected that Paul would exhort to the excommunication of *true* teachers. Nor is it said here that a church is authorized to excommunicate orderly and true ministers. If the church in Galatia was satisfied that these teachers were false, they had the right, it seems, to cut them off. So, in all time, churches that after trial convict ministers of crime can cut them off without any external assistance. Paul does not say, call a Presbytery to look into their ministerial credentials and expose them if they are impostors, or to take away their ministerial credentials if they have properly forfeited them,

and then exclude them from membership. But the exhortation is, cut them off.

3. Christ *praises* the church at Ephesus for excommunicating false apostles. "And thou hast tried them which say they are apostles, and are not, and hast found them liars." Rev. ii. 2. Now, these men professed to be apostles. So far as the church at Ephesus *knew*, they really were such, and, on investigation, their claims *might* have been sustained.

It did not follow that their claims were spurious simply because they were doubted. On this principle, Paul's apostleship would have been invalidated; for IT was called in question. The true state of the case was ascertained by investigation. The church tried them, and the church found them liars; and Christ praised her for it. Not one hint is given that she did this in co-operation with a Presbytery. If the church at Ephesus was *praised* for trying and cutting off false apostles, surely the Scriptures will sustain a church in modern times in trying and cutting off, in the same way, false ministers.

4. Peter, though he was an apostle, acknowledges the sole jurisdiction over him of the church in Jerusalem, of which he was a member. After the baptism of Cornelius, they of the circumcision at Jerusalem brought the charge against him that he had gone in to men uncircumcised, and eaten with them. Acts xi. We do not find that Peter claims to be tried by "his peers," and demands that a Council of Apostles, or

even of elders, should be called to decide upon the validity of his defence; but he expounds to the church the facts of the case, and seeks their approval of his conduct. I do not present this as technically an arraignment in the sense of church dealing, but only claim that Peter acknowledged that the church was able to decide upon the propriety of his course, and to acquit him of blame, without external assistance.

These instances appear to us to furnish decided evidence from the Scriptures that a minister can be tried, condemned, and expelled without the intervention of a Council or Presbytery.

Objection 1.—But, it is objected, "The ministry was conferred by a Presbytery or Council; and it requires the same power to unmake that it does to make."

To meet this objection, it will be necessary, as a preliminary, to inquire, 1. What is a minister? 2. What is ordination? 3. What relation does a Presbytery or Council bear to ordination?

1. *What is a minister?* A minister has two functions. 1st. He can preach the gospel; 2d. He can administer the ordinances of Baptism and the Lord's Supper.

1st. The first he does not possess as a prerogative peculiar to himself. All male members of the church have the right, and are in duty bound, to tell to others all they know about the Saviour. By conversation, or, if able, in set speech, sitting, walking, or standing, on the floor, or, if more convenient, in a pulpit, they are authorized to proclaim to sinners the unsearchable riches of Christ, and to point inquirers to the Lamb of God who taketh away the sins of the world; and this with all the impressiveness and eloquence at their command. "As every man hath received the gift, even so minister the same one to another, as good stewards of the manifold grace of God." 1 Peter iv. 10. But, while it is the privilege and duty of all to proclaim the truth, Christ has set apart a special body of men to the work of the ministry, as preachers, whose business it is to give themselves, with all their energies, to the proclamation of the truth,—to reprove, rebuke, and exhort, with all long-suffering and doctrine. A minister, then, in part, is one whose duty it is to preach the word.

2d. Some believe that any church-member is authorized to administer the ordinances; but, with very general unanimity, Baptists hold that only ordained ministers are authorized to do so. The answer, then, to the question, Who is a minister? is, One who preaches the gospel and administers the ordinances.

2. *What is ordination?* and what relation does it bear to the ministry?

Ans. 1st.—Whatever it may be, it does not impart any grace, or intellectual or spiritual qualification. There is no invisible gift imparted by the imposition of hands; nor does the ceremony bring the subject into a line of succession from the apostles, or make him a link in a ministerial chain from primitive times. This may do for Popery and High-Church Episcopacy, which depend upon superstition and credulity; but the Scriptures make no intimation of the necessity or the existence of such a line of succession. And if a Presbytery of Baptist ministers profess that ordination is designed, and that their manipulations are intended to bring a candidate into this mystical —not to say superstitious—line of succession, it may be well for them to be called upon to prove in advance that THEY are THEMSELVES in that line.

Ans. 2.—Ordination is not designed to AUTHORIZE the subject to preach. God gives that authority, and not the Presbytery. Men are ordained, not that they might become preachers, but because they are preachers already. God calls them to be such, bestows upon them the gifts and qualifications, rolls upon their hearts the burden of souls, kindles a fire in their bones, and compels them to cry, "Wo is me if I preach not the gospel." And when they prove themselves to be preachers, then the Presbyter lays hands on them, not that they might be preachers, but because they are so already. How many "licensed preachers" are there in our churches? Paul was called to be a preacher, and the call announced to Ananias, before his (Paul's) baptism,—to say nothing of ordination. (Acts ix. 15.) A head to know, a heart to feel, and a tongue to utter fluently and forcibly, the truth as it is in Jesus, are the qualifications that make the preacher, and not the external ceremony of ordination. These gifts and graces God bestows, and not the Presbytery. An ardent desire for the glory of God and for the salvation of sinners, and not the authorization of the Presbytery, is that which impels men to preach.

3. In answer, then, to the question, What is ordination? I would say, Ordination is, by ceremony, A SOLEMN PUBLIC RECOGNITION of one whom, it is believed, God has called to preach His gospel and administer His ordinances.

3. *What relation does a Presbytery bear to ordination?*—In other words, why is a Presbytery necessary to take a part in this solemn recognition?

Presbytery is derived from the Greek word *presbuteros*, and implies a company of elders or ministers In our churches in the Southern States, the ordain ing body is exclusively a company of ministers se lected by the candidate and the church to which h belongs. But in the Northern States it is customar for the church calling to ordination to invite neigh boring churches to send their pastors and messenger who shall together constitute what they call a Coun cil, to inquire into the propriety of ordaining th candidate. This latter body consists of priva members, as well as ministers. While this custo is liable to misconstruction, in the fact that it m be supposed that, as other churches send messengers to this body, the power to ordain belongs to an association of churches, it tends to correct a superstition which we are in danger of imbibing from Rome, that the body performing the ceremony of ordination communicate through themselves some spiritual gift, or, by virtue of being in that condition themselves, impart to the candidate ministerial succession, or make him, like themselves, a link in a ministerial chain from the apostles. The private members of these Councils are non-conductors of the ministerial fluid, and have not, in themselves, the ministerial succession to communicate. If it be said that not the private members of these Councils, but the ministers, lay hands on the subject, it is replied that the ministers do so, in part, by the permission and under the direction of the private members. In the mouth of a Romanist or a High-Church Episcopalian, apostolical succession, and ministerial qualification imparted by the laying on of hands, are superstitious and presumptuous; but in the mouth of a Baptist Council they are simply nonsensical and ridiculous. But to return.

Why is a Presbytery or a Council necessary to the solemn recognition of a minister? I answer, God designs (1) to prevent unworthy and incompetent men from entering into the ministry; and (2) to provide for the endorsement of worthy and competent men, so that they may be received with confidence by other churches and the world, who, for themselves, may not have the opportunity or ability to pass upon their character and qualifications. To secure the former, He makes the candidate pass through two ordeals. He has first, by his gifts and qualifications, to attract the attention of his church to himself, and convince it that God has called and qualified him for the work of the ministry; and then, having convinced the Presbytery or Council that he has gifts of mind and utterance that qualify him to edify, he must stand an examination before them which is conducted to see whether he has experienced a work of grace; what are his reasons for believing that God has called him into the ministry; what his motives for desiring to enter upon the work; and what are his views of Scripture doctrine and church order. If on any of these points he fails to give satisfaction, it is the duty of the Presbytery or Council to refuse to ordain him. And thus an unworthy or dangerous man fails to be turned loose to work mischief among the churches. If, however, on all these points the examination be satisfactory, they proceed to his ordination. In other words, by a solemn ceremony, well calculated to arrest attention, they, in concert with the church, declare to the world that, in their opinion, God has called this man to minister in holy things. This opinion they submit to writing, and place in the hands of the ordained, that it may be a testimony for him to the strangers among whom his lot may be cast, that, in the opinion of this church and these brethren composing the Presbytery or Council, God has called and qualified this man to be a minister of the New Testament.

Let us return now to the objection. I will repeat the words of it:—"The ministry was conferred by a Presbytery or Council; and it takes the same power to unmake that it does to make."

To this it is replied by denying that the Presbytery or Council CONFERS the office or MAKES the minister. All that they do is to RECOGNIZE and ENDORSE him as a minister. God, and not Presbyteries or Councils, makes ministers. Paul says, "I thank Christ Jesus our Lord, who hath enabled me, for that he counted me faithful, PUTTING ME INTO THE MINISTRY." 1 Tim. i. 12. To the latter part of the argument it is replied by denying that it takes always the same power to unmake that it does to make. The Ephesian Dome required many years and much treasure for its construction; but a madman and his torch consumed it in a few hours. A well established reputation requires long years of patient continuance in well-doing to build it up; for "confidence is a plant of slow growth." But one startling crime may, in a short hour, destroy it. So it takes many particulars to give confidence that one is a minister of Jesus Christ,—a renewed heart and faith in Christ; a knowledge and love of divine things; an utterance ready and forcible; an ardent desire to promote God's glory and the salvation of sinners; the conviction on the part of the church and Presbytery, or Council, that God has called and qualified him for the work; but one crime against religion and morality will, as soon as it is known, convince that all these evidences were deceptive. And, besides, if we were to grant that it takes the same power to unmake that it does to make, it is not pertinent here as an argument; for God alone makes ministers. If any interposition, then, is necessary, God, and not the Presbytery, is the power that must interpose. This interposition God does make, by investing His church with delegated sovereignty over ministers as well as others that are members, and encouraging it to "try them that say they are [ministers,] and are not," and to prove them "liars."

Objection 2.—It is objected again, "On your own principles, a Presbytery or Council was necessary in ordination to give the world confidence that, in the judgment of competent men, God designs the man to be a minister. On the strength of this endorsement, other churches and the world give him their confidence. Is not the same testimony necessary to authorize and induce them to withdraw that confidence?"

To this it is answered, it requires much stronger testimony, and that of different nature, to establish one's ministerial character and qualifications, than to show his unworthiness and crime. In the former, we need knowledge of the Scriptures, penetration into human character, renewed hearts of variety of disposition to appreciate the exposition of gospel truth,—in short, just such evidence as the concurrent testimony of a church of mixed members and a Presbytery of pious, intelligent, and experienced ministers can afford. But, in the latter, nothing is needed but the proof that he has been guilty of a crime against religion and morality. Now, a church is as able to investigate and pass upon the charge of crime alleged against a minister as the same alleged against any others of its members. And the testimony of her act in expelling him for falsehood, or adultery, or drunkenness, or any other great crime, needs no corroboration, and as effectually neutralizes and withdraws the testimony given in ordination, as though her act was concurred in by ten thousand Presbyteries.

Objection 3.—"The assertion of a right to try and expel a minister without a Presbytery, implies the assertion of the right on the part of the church to ordain a minister without a Presbytery. Now, if she were ordaining a man for herself exclusively, this might do; but, as ordination is designed to give him access as a minister to other churches also, and to the world at large, she cannot ordain him by herself, and, by parity of reasoning, she cannot depose him by herself."

To this I answer, Why is a church UNABLE to ordain one of her members herself? When the church at Jerusalem was the only one in existence, with the apostles in her membership, was she unable to ordain? At the present time, in this country, it is inexpedient for a church to do so; nay, I will go further, and say it is WRONG for her to do so; not, however, because the ordination would be invalid, but because it would not be influential. Ordination is designed as a solemn testimony, by those engaged in it, that, in their opinion, God has called this man and qualified him for the ministerial work. Now, Scripture and common sense teach that, to make this testimony influential, it must be above the suspicion of bias or incompetency. Whenever, therefore, a church at the present time, in the ordination of a minister, fails to fortify her testimony by the concurrent testimony of a Presbytery or Council, she gives evidence that there is something in the candidate's character or doctrinal belief which will prevent the approbation and endorsement of an honest, capable, and unbiassed Presbytery. So far, then, from her sole endorsement giving the ordained currency, it stamps him as spurious coin. We have a noted instance of this kind which has recently occurred in one of the Northern States. Even those who differ from me in the views expressed above, will grant that if a church has in her membership two ordained ministers besides her pastor, they, with the pastor, are competent to form an ordaining Presbytery; and if they admit that it would be inexpedient for the church to set apart to the ministry another of her members by the aid of such a Presbytery, they can explain that lack of expediency only upon the grounds upon which I have placed it, viz.: that it would not be sufficiently influential as an endorsement,—unless the ministers composing the Presbytery have an overshadowing reputation.

But the assertion of the right to try and expel a minister by the church alone, does not imply the assertion of the right to ordain him without the intervention of a Presbytery. The two ideas are not correlative. While the church may acknowledge that it is not so well able of itself to ascertain whether a candidate possesses ministerial grace and qualifications, and feels confident, therefore, that her sole endorsement will not be influential enough to give him circulation everywhere, it may assert, and the world may well grant to it, the right and the capacity to decide and act upon the crime committed by her member.

The church does not propose to ordain him for herself, any more than the churches which contributed members to the Council propose to ordain him for themselves; but only to endorse him as one worthy to be received as a minister everywhere, and qualified to be the pastor of any church that may wish HIS services. Ordination does not make a man a pastor, or give him official relations to any church. There are many ordained ministers that have no pastoral or other official relations to a church.

Objection 4.—"But ought not a man to be tried by his peers?"

I answer, Yes. But the members of the church

constitute his peers. "One is your master, and all ye are brethren." Were a minister to be tried before the courts of the country on a criminal charge, likely as not, the jury of his peers that would sit upon his case would be a petit jury, composed of individuals not distinguished for their intelligence or moral worth. But do you mean by "his peers" his colleagues in office? If so, and your principles be right, then should all Deacons under charges be tried by a Council of Deacons!

It would seem, then, that it must be granted that ministers, like others, are subject to the churches to which they belong; and that, should they be guilty of crime, the church, in the exercise of delegated sovereignty, can arraign them, try them, and expel them, without the intervention of Presbyteries or Councils.

So much would I say in regard to the RIGHTS of the churches. I would not be understood, however, to maintain that a church, in dealing with her minister, CANNOT call in the aid of a Council; nor to intimate that in many instances it would not be HIGHLY JUDICIOUS to do so.

CHAPTER IX.

DEDUCTIONS (CONTINUED)—CHURCH INDEPENDENCE.

Deduction 2.—*The decision of the church is final.* "If he neglect to hear the church, let him be to thee as an heathen man and a publican."

The admission has been incautiously made by good writers on the subject of discipline that in extreme cases, where it is evident that gross injustice has been done, one church may receive to membership the excluded member of another. They all plead, though, that it must be an extreme case, and recommend to the use of great caution in the exercise of what they call the right,—a recommendation, however, that is never observed; for it is only in cases involving extreme excitement that there is any temptation to take such a step.

Baptists boast that they have a "thus saith the Lord" for all their principles and practices. They claim that on the subject of doctrinal faith and church order the New Testament is profitable for doctrine, for reproof, for correction, and for instruction in righteousness; and that, with this manual in their hands, they are perfect, thoroughly furnished unto all good works. In the matter of the discipline and expulsion of a disorderly member, the New Testament is plain and explicit. Is it silent on the subject of excommunicated persons? Does it lead us through a path flooded with light to the point of their excommunication, and then leave us profoundly in the dark as to their relations, if any, to the church expelling, and as to the means of their restoration to the ranks of Christ's disciples, should they desire it? It would be strange were this so. The New Testament is not thus silent; and to a candid inquirer it gives an answer plain and unmistakable. That answer is, that the action of the church is final; that one church cannot receive to membership the excluded members of another; and that such excluded members can be restored to fellowship only by the action of the church expelling them. This I am prepared to show:—

1. BY POSITIVE PRECEPT. 2. BY INSPIRED EXAMPLE. 3. BY GENERAL PRINCIPLES LAID DOWN IN THE SCRIPTURES.

1. We have a precept, *first*, as to what is to be done with the incorrigible under each class of offences; and, *second*, as to our feelings and deportment towards those who have received the penalty prescribed.

First. If, in a personal offence, the offender refuse to give reparation to the one trespassed upon; if he decline to listen to the remonstrances of the one or two disinterested brethren who labour with him; and, finally, if he neglect to hear the church, he is to be withdrawn from. I suppose all will grant that this is in accordance with the Scriptures. If any one that is called a brother be convicted of a gross crime against religion and morality; as, for instance, if he be a fornicator, or covetous, or an idolater, or a drunkard, or an extortioner, the precept is, "Put away from among yourselves that wicked person." Here all is clear; and there is no room to doubt. A private offender that cannot be brought to repentance and reparation, and a gross public offender, are, according to the precept, to be excommunicated. But this is not all the instruction we receive on the subject from the Scriptures. We are told,—

Second, What are to be our feelings and deportment towards the excommunicated? Do we ask the Saviour what relations do we sustain towards one cut off for incorrigible wrong towards his brother? His answer is, "Let him be unto thee as an heathen man and a publican." Do we address the same inquiry to the great Apostle of the Gentiles in regard to offenders of every type? We have, in effect, the same reply: "Now I beseech you, brethren, *mark them* which cause divisions and offences contrary to the doctrine which ye have learned, and avoid them." Rom. xvi. 17. "Now I have written unto you not to keep company" with them. 1 Cor. v. 11. "Now we command you, brethren, in the name of our Lord Jesus Christ, that ye withdraw yourselves from every brother that walketh disorderly." 2 Thess. iii. 6. In regard to the disposition a church should make of a disorderly member, and the relations all churches and church-members bear to him when thus disposed of, the Scriptures are plain and explicit. He is to be excommunicated; and all are to withdraw themselves from him, to keep no company with him, to avoid him, and to make him bear towards them the relations of an heathen man and a publican. Now, whatever may be the meaning of these precepts when carried out into practice in detail, no one will maintain that in them can be found encouragement or authority for one church to receive the excluded member of another. Every one must grant that they, by strong implication, forbid such interference. These precepts are enough; but they do not constitute all the support that the Scriptures furnish to our position.

2. *Scripture example* shows that the excommunicating church alone can restore to membership. But one example is given in the Scriptures of the exclusion and restoration of a member. The incestuous man at Corinth was, at the instance of Paul, excommunicated; and when he had given satisfactory evidence of repentance and reformation, at the solicitation of Paul, he was restored to membership by the same church. There was a large number of

others in existence at that time besides the church at Corinth. Paul was not compelled, therefore, to apply to it because it was the only one extant. Now, Baptists claim that inspired *example* is as binding as inspired precept. In this way alone do they discover the form and organization of a gospel church. Nowhere in the New Testament is to be found a precept containing a rule for the organization and government of a gospel church. For our ideas and our practices upon these subjects, we are dependent exclusively upon inspired *example*. And in no instance do we reason against our Pedobaptist friends more forcibly and conclusively than when we maintain the binding force of New Testament example. Now, can we be honest when we denounce others for disregarding inspired example in the organization and government of the church, if we refuse to receive that same example as binding on any other subject? We ask, How can an expelled man be restored to membership? and are answered, by New Testament example, that he is to be restored by the same church that expelled him, after satisfaction rendered. Now, if we decline to receive the answer, while we sin against God, we lay ourselves open to the retort from our Pedobaptist friends, "Physician, heal thyself." Inspired precept *and* example, then, forbid one church to receive the excommunicated members of another, and declare that, when a church expels, her action is final. Nor is this all.

3. The *general principles* laid down in the Scriptures forbid one church to receive the excommunicated members of another. Let the following be noted:—

1st. All the churches are under Christ's jurisdiction. He is their Sovereign, and upon Him are they dependent. He gives the form of their organization, furnishes the regenerated materials of which they are to be composed, prescribes the laws by which they are to be governed, and fixes the relations they are to sustain to each other. Christ is the great King in Zion, and of Him no church is independent. Now, if this be true, the church cannot say, "I am independent, and I will do what I please;" but "Christ is my Sovereign, and I will do what He commands or permits." Now, Christ does not command or authorize one church to receive the excommunicates of another, but by precepts and example forbids it to do so. The first general principle I lay down, then, is, that the church, not only in its organization, duties, and rights, but also in its relations to other churches, is just what Christ, the Sovereign, makes it. This needs no proof.

2. Christ has constituted every church independent,—not of Himself, but of other churches. This all grant. Now, the question is, What is the meaning of independence? I have already said, it means *freedom from control*. A State is independent of other States when it is free from their control. So

a church is independent of other churches because, in like manner, it is free from their control. Now, if it can be shown that the reception of the excluded member of a church is an attempt to control it in its internal affairs, it will be evident from this general principle of the Scriptures that such an act is forbidden. Nothing is easier than to show that such an interference is a total subversion of church independence. If the church at A. can, without her consent, give membership to a man whom the church at B. excludes, whatever may be said of the independence of A., that of B. has been subverted; for she has been involuntarily *controlled* in her discipline by the interference of A. Is it said that A. does not interfere with B., since she takes one that has no connection with her? I answer, she just as unequivocally takes away B.'s member as though she had entered into the church and forcibly removed him while his trial was progressing, and before sentence of excommunication had been passed. The design of corrective discipline, even in its highest censures, is not to injure, but to reform. The Scriptures command the church to excommunicate a disorderly member, *that he might be brought to repentance and reformation.* They require it, "To deliver such an one to Satan for the destruction of the flesh, *that the spirit may be saved in the day of the Lord Jesus.*" 1 Cor. v. 5. "If any man obey not our word by this epistle, note that man, and have no company with him, *that he may be ashamed.*" 2 Thess. iii. 14. Now, the church at B., in obedience to the commands of the King in Zion, is pursuing a course of discipline designed to bring the offender to his senses; but midway in the process, just as soon as the regimen begins to take effect, A. interferes and rescues from her jurisdiction her excluded *member.* For he is still her member, with the descriptive prefix, *excluded.* From *rights* and *privileges* in the church he is "cut off," and as it regards *fellowship* and *fraternity* he is as an heathen man and a publican; but in relation to the discipline of the church he is still the subject of her reformatory process. Her disciplinary grasp upon him can never be relaxed until he reforms or dies. Now, this act of A. is just as decided an interference as though she had interposed at the instant of the arraignment, or at any time during the progress of the trial, before the final result. The discipline is never complete until it brings the culprit to repentance and reformation. When, therefore, the church at A. successfully interferes with the attempt of B. to bring the offender to a sense of his wrong, she just as effectually *controls the discipline* of B. as though she had dragged the arraigned from her bar. Had she done the latter, she would have protected him from *trial;* if she does the former, she rescues him from the intended *effect* of the discipline. Surely, if brethren will reflect, they need not wait for it to be proved to them by argument that their proposed action is designed to be an *interference.*

The reception of an individual into the membership of a church, and his expulsion from that same fellowship, are not "correlative" or "commensurate" ideas. Before he is received, he bears *no relation* to the church; but when he is expelled, he sustains the relation of one who is the subject of its reformatory discipline. He has passed through the discipline of *remonstrance* and *trial,* and is now the subject of the discipline of *correction* and *reformation.* This proposition seems to be very plain; but it receives additional support from the fact that such an one can never be received again in the same way as he was from the world at first. *Then,* he was *admitted* by experience and baptism; *now,* he must be not admitted, but restored, according to the Scriptures, by satisfaction rendered, without baptism. Expulsion does not leave a man in the same condition that reception found him. Therefore, reception and expulsion are not commensurate ideas nor correlative terms. The expelled man is still the subject, in a sense, of the church expelling him; and its discipline, which is designed to reform him, is just beginning on him its salutary influences. Now, this power and duty Christ conferred upon each church; and, that it might effectually feel the obligation and exercise the power, He made it independent of all others,—in other words, made it free from their interference or control. When one thus interferes, then it exercises not a right, but a usurpation; it shows not independence, but lawlessness. Do you ask me, in reply, "Is every church bound by the action of others." Without stopping to expose the fallacy contained in the word "bound," I reply, every church is bound to obey the commands of the Master; and *they* prohibit it to interfere with the internal discipline of its neighbors.

It is the Saviour's design not to envelop the earth in the folds of one vast hierarchy, but to dot its surface with local organizations, each having independent jurisdiction within its restricted territories, and all responsible to Him, the great King in Zion. This has been forcibly illustrated by reference to our county courts. The territory of the county constitutes the limits of its jurisdiction, the people of the county the subjects of its administration. When one tribunal arraigns one of its subjects before its bar, he cannot be removed from its jurisdiction by any process from another; and when it condemns and sentences him, he cannot appeal to another for relief. Why? Because they are independent of each other, but are all subject to a superior power, viz.: the organic law of the State, which marks out the limits of their jurisdiction severally, and the extent of their responsibility. If the circuit court of Clarke County interfere successfully with that of Oglethorpe, it not only destroys the independence of the latter, but it rebels against the constitution and law of the State. So when one church arrests another in the enforcement of its discipline, and removes away from the condemned the censure which was designed to work his reformation, she not only subverts the independence of the latter, but shows rebellion against the authority of Christ, who marks out the metes and bounds of their jurisdictions, and responsibilities severally, and makes them all mutually independent, *i.e.* free from each other's control. Independence, then, so far from authorizing, forbids one church to receive the excommunicated members of another.

3. But, again, in the exercise of his sovereign prerogative, Christ not only established the rights and duties of each church, but He settled the relations they are to sustain to each other, and the bonds by which they are to be united. He not only made them independent in their own jurisdictions, but He united them together by the bond of *Christian union*. He prays His Father that they all may be one; in faith, in love, in effort. His design is that no root of bitterness should spring up between them, to trouble, to distract, and to divide. Now, can it be believed that He who is infinitely wise should desire and pray for their Christian union, and yet should so organize them,—should invest them with such prerogative as, if exercised, will produce, inevitably, antagonism, alienation, and heart-burning?

No church can arbitrarily rescue a member from the jurisdiction of another, and welcome him into her fold, without destroying fellowship and Christian union. This Christian union Christ intended to exist between His churches; and, in infinite wisdom, He adapted the means to the end. He could not, therefore, have designed that one should arbitrarily overrule the decisions or recklessly trample upon the feelings of another. For the same reason, He could not have intended that one should receive to fellowship the excommunicated member of another.

We have given the teachings of the Scriptures on the subject. By direct precept, by plain example, and by unmistakable general principles, they teach us that an excluded man can in no way be restored to fellowship but by the action of the church expelling him. Shall we not accept this as satisfactory? Shall we rather attempt to settle the question by appeals to expediency and convenience? If so, then let our mouths be shut when Pedobaptists make a like appeal to expediency and convenience in regard to church organization and government, or gospel ordinances.

But brethren who oppose these views present plausible pleas by way of objection. These I would classify as:—1. *The plea explanatory;* 2. *The plea from expediency;* and, 3. *The plea from exceptional cases.* Let us consider them.

1. THE PLEA EXPLANATORY. They say, "We do

not claim that one church has the right to restore an excluded man to membership in the church expelling him, but only, by virtue of its independence, to receive him into its own. This certainly is no interference." To this I answer,—

1st. You do restore him to the fellowship of the church expelling, or else you destroy Christian union. Christian union remaining between the two churches, whenever the table of the Lord is spread, he, as well as other members of your church, can sit down to it, though formally excluded from it by vote of the body; and whenever he is present at the "conference" of the church, he can accept the usual invitations, dictated by Christian union, to take seats and aid in deliberations. Through your action, the excluding church will either be compelled to make to him all the expressions of Christian fellowship, though it has professed to withdraw it from him, or else to withdraw fellowship from you; and thus Christian union will be destroyed. But,—

2d. Your act will certainly be an interference with its discipline, as has been already shown; since it is designed to prevent the intended *effect* of that discipline.

2. THE PLEA FROM EXPEDIENCY. It is said, "It is a great hardship for one to be unjustly expelled; and surely there ought to be a remedy for it. If the church perpetrating the injustice cannot be induced

to repair the injury, surely other churches ought to be at liberty to remedy the evil."

Ah! You would then propose to supply the defects in the enactments of the Lawgiver! But how do you propose to counteract the evil? I answer, by introducing a greater. At present, one individual suffers. This you propose to remedy by the introduction of an expedient that would destroy Christian union between two churches, and thus produce discord, confusion, and division. This is bad enough, when union is destroyed between two churches alone. How much, though, is the evil enhanced when the rescued is a professed minister! If he permits you to restore him, he is influenced by a spirit of resistance to the church expelling him. The same spirit of resistance will lead him to seek expressions of fellowship and endorsement from as wide an extent of country as possible, and from all such religious bodies as can, either directly or indirectly, indicate such fellowship. And thus we shall have presented to us the strange spectacle of a religious demagogue, under your sanction, traveling over the country soliciting support and gathering to himself a party. Wherever he goes, he will find some who reverence the authority of the King in Zion, and who are compelled, therefore, to treat him as an excommunicated man. His presence introduces divisions and heart-burnings into every church whose majority receives him as a minister. Wherever he goes, he has his own feelings injured by the words and actions of the faithful men who dare to abide by the law of Christ. Thus, you do not alleviate, but increase, his sufferings; and you make him the wedge which you drive home to the rending apart of the people of God over a vast district. Surely, it is not expedient to attempt to remedy a limited evil by the application of another so great and unlimited. And, besides, it will be all in vain. The man you propose to protect cannot maintain the position your sympathy and his resentment assign him. He will either be permitted by God's providence to go to such lengths as to make you ashamed of the support you have given him, or else he will see his error and return back from whence he departed. If he is a Christian, this latter will be the inevitable result. There is too much faithfulness to Christ in the great Baptist heart, and too much knowledge of the Scriptures in the Baptist mind, for them to be long misled. He must either come back whence he departed, or else come to nought. This is the history of all such cases. Happy will it be for him and for Christian union in the churches if his rebellion be of short continuance. When you see that such will be the deplorable results, tell me not that your action is designed, in the fear of God, to counteract evil. Ascribe it rather to amiable weakness, to sympathy, to wilfulness, to partisanship, to personal resentment,—to any thing, rather than to a regard for the authority of God's law or the honor of God's cause.

3. THE PLEA FROM EXCEPTIONAL CASES. It is asked, "Suppose a church should expel a member for joining the Masons or Odd-Fellows, or another should expel its member for favoring the missionary cause, or, if he is a minister, for maintaining that the gospel is to be preached to sinners: will it not be lawful in these cases, or in either of them, for a neighboring church to receive the excluded? Now, if you answer in the affirmative, you, in effect, give up the principle; for you acknowledge that, for sufficient cause, one church may receive the expelled of another."

To answer this question, it must be analyzed and the parts classified under different heads.

1. One church expels its member for doing that which the Scriptures do not in terms forbid, but which they do not require him to do. A member joins the Masons or Odd-Fellows, not because he feels bound to do so conscientiously, in the fear of God, from a sense of duty, but because he deems it expedient and feels inclined to do so.

2. The other church expels its member for practicing that which he and we believe to be enjoined in the Scriptures. He acts from a sense of duty and in the fear of God, and does just what we conscientiously believe it is his duty to do. Now, you per-

ceive, we must give very different answers to these questions. Let us take them up separately.

1. If a church expels one for joining the Masons or Odd-Fellows, is it lawful for a neighboring church to receive him? I answer, No. I have not a word to say in disparagement of these highly respectable institutions; and I grant that I can see nothing sinful in becoming connected with them. But then it is the duty of a church-member to seek the harmony and brotherly union of his church when he can do so without sacrificing his conscience. Paul said that all things were lawful, but all things were not expedient for him. Though it was lawful for him to eat meat, he announced it as his determination never to do so while the world would stand, if it would cause his brother to offend. Some of the best brethren we have in the land are those who were Masons before their conversion, or who became so afterward without being aware of the strong objections—or prejudices, if you please—of their brethren. But as soon as they became aware of the opposition, they consented to discontinue their attendance upon the Lodge. They esteemed their church privileges higher than their relations to any worldly associations, however honorable and useful. And they stood ready to sever any relation dictated merely by expediency and convenience, rather than destroy the peace of a church composed—if you please—of only ignorant and weak brethren. Now, when a

member allows himself to be expelled on this ground, it is because he is headstrong, because he offends against charity, and because he esteems that which is merely expedient to him of more value than the peace of the church and the confidence and affection of his brethren. A simple promise to discontinue his attendance on the Lodge will remove all the difficulty. Now, if the church, proposing to reverse the sentence of expulsion, conscientiously believes that it is the duty of every individual, in the fear of God, to join the Masons, and makes this profession a part of its creed, if it professes that this, as an obligation, is enjoined in the Scriptures, it may then receive the member, because it can at the same time withdraw from the expelling church on the ground that it professes rebellion to God by refusing to join the Masons and by prohibiting its members to do so. A church, in conscientiously expelling a Mason, may act very foolishly; but her evil cannot be removed by the introduction of a greater,—viz., the destruction of church union,—unless you are prepared to withdraw fellowship from her for maintaining that Masons should be expelled. This is a case that calls not for anathemas, but for light. "Him that is weak in the faith receive ye, but not to doubtful disputations."

2. But when a church expels a member for favoring the missionary cause or for preaching the gospel to sinners, *it* is clearly of a different denomination

from us, or has so departed from the faith as to authorize us to withdraw fellowship from it. In that case, church sovereignty is not violated if we receive those who are martyrs to the same truth we conscientiously hold ourselves. The principle here is that which I avowed in a previous number,— that when a church ceases to be a Baptist church we may withdraw fellowship from it. But you observe that this principle is not operative in a case in which we receive one excluded by a church professing to be of the same faith and order,—one who was arraigned and tried upon such charges as, if they had been proved upon him, would have made him, in our opinion, worthy of expulsion. The church must not only appear to us to act in opposition to what we consider the law of Christ, but it must avow that to be its intention, before we can be authorized to withdraw fellowship from it and afford a refuge to its excluded members. A mere difference of opinion from us in the interpretation of a law of Christ which it professes to hold as tenaciously as we—the law in Matt. xviii., if you please—cannot be sufficient ground with us for declaring it to be no longer a Baptist church. Who gave to us such infallibility as to make our interpretations of Scripture always unerringly right? And whence do we obtain the arrogance which authorizes us to deny all ecclesiastical claims to any body that may differ from us in opinion? The "Primitive Baptists' have declared non-fellowship for us because we maintain boards and conventions for promoting missions. They have, in effect, declared themselves a denomination distinct from us. When, therefore, we take them on their own terms, and receive those of their members who have been excluded for conscientiously maintaining the same truths on whose account we ourselves have been withdrawn from, we violate no church comity, we disturb no Christian union.

It is always best for us to be governed by Scripture instruction, however great may be the injustice done us or our friend, and however much we may be excited in consequence. And the Scriptures—by precepts, by examples, and by general principles—assure us that, if an excommunicated man be restored at all, he must be restored by the church that expelled him.

Question 1.—"May not the expelled member who thinks himself unjustly treated find relief by appealing to his Association or to a Council?"

I answer, The Scriptures recognize no such bodies as Associations and Councils. The church is the highest and the only ecclesiastical body known to the New Testament. Some have endeavored to find the germ of Associations and Councils in the meeting held in Jerusalem by the apostles, elders, and brethren, to consider and to give advice on the matters of difficulty presented by the church at Antioch. But this only shows how easy it is to pervert the plain and common-sense transactions of apostolic times to the purposes of superstition, and to the acquisition of materials for the foundation of an unscriptural hierarchy. The Jerusalem Church was the first planted by the apostles, and, therefore, the Mother Church. Now, certain men, which came down from Judea, taught the brethren at Antioch, that except they be circumcised after the manner of Moses they could not be saved. These sentiments were vehemently opposed by Paul and Barnabas. But when the church at Antioch found they were not able to settle the question, they sent Paul and Barnabas and certain others to Jerusalem to inquire of the church, and the apostles and elders, whether these men properly represented their sentiments, and what was their opinion on the subject. The whole multitude assembled together, and, under the guidance of the Holy Spirit, repudiated these teachers, and solved the difficulty. This was a simple and common-sense transaction. Nothing is more natural than the inquiry, and nothing more natural than the means adopted to answer it. But here was no permanent body, composed of messengers from contiguous churches, to meet at stated times, organized upon a written constitution, and called an "Association;" nor a transient body, composed in like manner of messengers from churches, and called a "Council." It was simply a meeting of the whole church with the apostles and elders then in Jerusalem. But suppose it be granted that Associations and Councils are modeled after the same form and organized for the same purpose. The meeting in Jerusalem assembled to give advice to a church which had asked it, and this, too, not on a case of discipline, but on a point of doctrine. It received and entertained no appeal from a man under dealing.

Associations are institutions of modern date. They are not opposed to the general principles of the Scriptures; and as advisory councils, and a means of promoting Christian union and co-operation,—if they refrain scrupulously from infringing upon the internal rights of the churches, and from lording it over God's heritage,—they may be made to subserve a valuable purpose. But it is not necessary for the completeness of a church that it should be a member of such a body. One of the most ominous signs of the times, and a marked indication of a disposition on the part of these bodies to transcend their legitimate bounds, is a resolution passed in the meetings of some of them, inviting ministers to seats who are in good standing in their own churches *and Associations*. This implies that, if the minister's church belongs to no association, his ecclesiastical relations are incomplete. On this principle, Paul and all the other apostles, if present, would be ruled out as undeserving a seat, because of their defective ecclesiastical relations. In what respect does this differ in principle from Presbyterianism? There, the minister is not in full connection because he does not belong to a Presbytery; here, he is defective because he is not in Associational connection. Are these bodies blind and unconscious of the claim implied here? or are they fully aware of its extent? If the latter be true, how long will it take for the churches to become mere societies and component parts of an unscriptural hierarchy, fast approximating to the organization of "The Man of Sin"? So impossible is it to avoid sounding the profound abyss of error, when unscriptural expedients are used to counteract what we consider injustice and oppression! An Association may give a church advice in regard to scriptural *principles* when it asks it, which advice it may follow, or not, as it thinks best; but an Association may never interfere, directly or indirectly, with the internal affairs of a church, nor listen to the appeals of its member whom it is making the subject of its discipline.

When a church needs assistance in the management of a case of discipline, it may ask the aid of contiguous churches. These may appoint their wisest men, who may together constitute a COUNCIL, or, as it is sometimes called, a COMMITTEE OF HELPS. These may attend upon the meeting of the church, and, after hearing the case, may give her the benefit of their mature judgment, leaving it to her to receive or reject their opinion, as to her may seem best. They may never authoritatively decide a case, nor obtrude their advice when it is not asked. None but a church can call them into being, and when they perform the office the church assigns them, they are dissolved again into their original elements. If the church asks their aid in a case of discipline, to the best of their ability, they may render it; but they can never take the case out of the hands of the church. Least of all can they arraign the church, and sit in judgment on its acts. They are a mere advisory body; and after the church hears their advice, it may reject it and go counter to it, and nobody will have any right to complain. It never can be a body to whom an appeal can be taken from the church; nor can it ever owe its existence to a member under discipline, nor to a minority of the church. "We have no such custom, neither the churches of God." A member unjustly expelled, then, can find no relief from a Council; for such a body cannot exist, according to Baptist usage, except it be created by the church.

Question 2.—"But may not churches err?"

To this I answer, ten thousand times, yes. More frequently, however, by retaining unworthy members than by expelling the worthy. How often are members tolerated in covetousness which is idolatry; in frequenting improper places of amusement; in quaffing the inebriating cup, till some of them die, church-members, with delirium tremens; and in the indulgence of an improper spirit, and the utterance of improper language toward their brethren! Where one is unjustly expelled, hundreds are sinfully retained in church connection. If God has aught against his churches, as to discipline, it is for their neglect in enforcing it, rather than for their reckless and cruel execution of it.

Question 3.—"What remedy, then, has one conscious of unjust expulsion?"

I answer again, none, according to the Scriptures, excepting from the church expelling him. But then, if she is unrelenting, or tardy in her return to justice,—

1. An opportunity is afforded him to submit humbly to the will of God. He knows that God's will of purpose is frequently accomplished through the ignorance or wickedness of men. Even the crucifixion of Christ, that event ordained by infinite Grace, was brought about by the wicked action of wicked men. "Him, being delivered by the determinate counsel and foreknowledge of God, ye have taken, and by wicked hands have crucified and slain." God's way is in the sea, and his path in the great waters. And though it is inscrutable to him, he sees by the event that it is the Lord's will that he should be an excommunicated man. He knows that his Father, who has promised that all things shall work together for his good, has some wise purpose to accomplish in him or by him; and his lan-

guage is, "The will of the Lord be done." However great may be the outrage he suffers, and however trying to the flesh its infliction, he is more than compensated if it is sanctified to bring him, like a little child, unmurmuringly and uncomplainingly, at the feet of the Infinite Sovereign.

2. If he has been mistreated because of his principles, an opportunity is afforded him to suffer as a martyr for the truth. The primitive disciples did not esteem it an intolerable hardship thus to suffer. *They* "rejoiced that they were counted worthy to suffer shame for his name." One thus meekly suffering for such a cause knows, by experience, what the Saviour meant when He said, "Blessed are ye when men shall revile you and persecute you, and say all manner of evil against you falsely for my sake." And he can "rejoice and be exceeding glad," knowing that "great is his reward in heaven." Nor need he have any fear that scriptural principles will be overthrown by his fall; for he knows that "the blood of the martyrs is the seed of the church."

3. If his brethren have acted through misapprehension, it remains for him to show, by a well-ordered life and a godly conversation, that they have misunderstood him. If they have wilfully mistreated him, he can wait patiently in hope that God's providence and grace, and the quiet operation of outside public opinion, will revolutionize opinions in the

church and bring it right. But if the worst comes, he has the consolation to know,—

4. That expulsion from the church is not expulsion from the kingdom of heaven. His brethren, through mistake, or wickedly, have erased his name from the church-book; but by infinite grace it stands recorded on the Lamb's book of life. He is cut off from communion with those with whom he was wont to take sweet counsel; but his fellowship is still with the Father, and with His Son, Jesus Christ. He is denied any further membership with God's visible people; but the church universal recognizes his right to membership. God has given him a position in that glorious company; and no earthly power can deprive him of it. Regenerated by God's Spirit and called by His grace, kept by His power and guided by His counsel, he will ultimately be received into glory, where he shall be welcomed to sit down with Abraham, Isaac, and Jacob, and all the Apostles and Prophets, in the General Assembly and church of the first-born that are written in heaven. His brethren may avoid him, or view him with repulsive or lowering looks; but he basks in the smiles of God's countenance, and Christ is to him a friend that sticketh closer than a brother. Men may say that he is not worthy of a name among God's people; but the heavenly comforter bears witness with his Spirit that he is a child of God, and gives him the spirit of adoption, by which he can say, Abba, Father.

And when, driven near to God by these afflictions, he attains to the full assurance of faith,—when, trusting only in Christ, he makes his calling and election sure,—condemned though he is by frail and erring mortals, he can adopt for himself the exulting language of the apostle, "Who shall separate me from the love of Christ? Shall tribulation, or distress, or persecution, or famine, or nakedness, or peril, or sword? Nay, in all these things I am more than a conqueror through him that loved me. For I am persuaded that neither death, nor life, nor angels, nor principalities, nor powers, nor things present, nor things to come, nor height, nor depth, nor any other creature, shall be able to separate me from the love of God which is in Christ Jesus my Lord."

THE END.

A
BIOGRAPHICAL SKETCH
OF
PATRICK HUES MELL
(1814-1888)

BY
JOHN FRANKLIN JONES

A Biographical Sketch of Patrick Hues Mell (1814-1888)

Patrick Hues Mell—educator, preacher, country pastor, college professor, theologian, author, denominational leader, parliamentarian, Civil War soldier/officer—was born in Walthourville (Cathcart), Liberty County, Georgia, July 19, 1814 to Benjamin and Cynthia Sumner Mell. His father died when Patrick was fourteen, his mother when he was only sixteen or seventeen, from which time this eldest son provided means of support for his siblings (*ESB*).

Mell was baptized at North Newport church, Liberty County, Georgia in the summer of 1832 by Rev. Samuel Law. After studying in the academies in Liberty County and near Darien (Cathcart), Mell borrowed money and entered Amherst College, Massachusetts, where he matriculated from 1833-35 (*ESB*). He taught in the academy at Springfield, Massachusetts and high school at East Hartford, Connecticut. At twenty-four he returned to Georgia to teach school in the middle and lower parts of the state for five or six years (Cathcart).

He began to preach at Oxford, Georgia in 1840 and was ordained at and by the Penfield church at the request of the Greensborough church November 19, 1842 (Cathcart). He served the Greensborough church as pastor for ten years. He became pastor of the Bairdstown church, Greene County, Georgia, in 1848, and the Antioch church, Oglethorpe County, Georgia in January 1852, serving both churches simultaneously for a while. He served the Antioch church for twenty-six years (until 1878) (Mell, *LPHM*, 54-55).

His preaching was logical and argumentative, deeply doctrinal in its biblical content, yet simple and clearly comprehended. Powerful and keen in his intellect and skilled in thinking and reasoning, he presented divine truth forcibly and clearly (Cathcart).

Mell became professor of Ancient Languages at Mercer University in February 1842 and continued therein till November 1855. He became Professor of Ancient Languages at the State University in Athens in August 1856, was elected to the chair of Metaphysics and Ethics in 1860, and in August 1878, elected chancellor of the university and ex-officio president of the State College of Agriculture and Mechanic Arts (Cathcart).

Furman University conferred upon him the D.D. degree in 1858. Howard College conferred upon him the LL.D degree in 1869 (*ESB*).

Mell served as president of the Southern Baptist Convention 1863-71 and 1880-87 (*ESB*). The esteem with which Southern Baptists held him is indicated in the number of times they elected him as their president—fifteen times--more than any other president. Only two other men--James P. Boyce & Jonathan Haralson—even approximated that number of elections, each being elected nine times (*2000 Annual*). He presided over the George Baptist Convention from 1857 to 1864. He moderated the Georgia Baptist Association for 31 years (*ESB*).

An able writer, Mell published several works addressing varied subjects. Larger works addressed baptism, church discipline, and parliamentary practice. At his death he was working on a volume on Baptist church polity (*ESB*). Smaller works were written about slavery, predestination, Calvinism,

A Biographical Sketch of Patrick Hues Mell

God's providential government, and philosophy of prayer (Cathcart).

When Mell became pastor at Antioch, the church had, for some time, been disturbed by difficulty. In a few short months, however, its peace was restored. Shortly thereafter, a meeting was scheduled. Continuing for two weeks or longer, the meeting was a great success. Baptisms occurred almost daily, at which Mell would expound a Scripture touching the ordinance.

Enjoyed by and instructive to his people, the sermons aroused considerable animus among the Pedobaptists. From that stirring came a discussion on Scriptural baptism with the Methodist minister at Centre, Rev. Parks. Afterwards, Mell's congregations at Bairdstown and Antioch requested that he publish the sermons. The result was his *Baptism in Its Mode and Subjects* (1854). Widely circulated, the book occasioned the conversion of several Pedobaptists to the Baptist faith and practice (Mell, *LPHM*, 55-56).

Mell penned *Predestination and the Saints' Perseverance, Stated and Defended from the Objections of Arminians, in a Review of Two Sermons, Published by Rev. Russell Reneau.* The foreword was dated December 1850 at Mercer University, but the formal publication date is obscure. He wrote this logical and biblical defense of the Calvinistic schemes of predestination and perseverance in response to the poorly- and weakly-argued rantings of an Arminian contemporary preacher, Russell Reneau.

A long-time member of the Antioch church, Mrs. D. B. Fitzgerald (Miss Mary E. Crowley) spoke kindly and lovingly of Mell as her pastor. Also noting the confusion of the church at the initiation of Mell's tenure as pastor, Mrs. Fitzgerald identified the problem as a theological one–the church was drifting into the error of Arminianism. Relative to this issue, she wrote of Mell:

He loved the truth too well to blow hot and cold with the same breath. If it was a *Baptist* [italics in original] church it must have doctrines peculiar to that denomination preached to it. And with that boldness, clearness and vigor of speech that marked him, he preached to them the doctrines of predestination, election, free-grace, etc." (Mell, *LPHM*, 59).

The brief work, *An Exposition of Recent Events*, exposed the 1855 ex parte actions of the Board of Mercer University severing Mell from that institution His son provided additional details regarding the events surrounding the departure of the elder Mell from that institution and the ensuring controversy across Georgia (Mell, *LPHM*).

Corrective Church Discipline (1860) was the book form of his series of articles appearing in state Baptist papers 1859-60 on the subject. Stirred over the J. R. Graves controversy in the First Baptist Church of Nashville and questioning the wisdom of that church's expulsion of Graves et al., a number of leaders requested Mell to address questions over the status of members in the church, the jurisdiction of the churches, and the relations between the churches and associations in such matters (Mell, *LPHM*, 108) .

Mell was an excellent parliamentarian. Known as the "prince of parliamentarians, his skill at presiding is published in *A Manual of Parliamentary Practice* (ca. 1867). He also wrote a short work on prayer--*The Doctrine of Prayer* (ca. 1876) (*ESB*).

In the later civil war, he raised a company of troops at the call of the governor and was elected their captain. When the regiment was organized, he was elected colonel and served actively for six months at differing points in the state (Cathcart).

Mell was married twice. His first wife, Lurene Howard Cooper, Montgomery County, Georgia, was the daughter of

A Biographical Sketch of Patrick Hues Mell

George Cooper. To this first marriage union were born nine children: five sons and four daughters. Five were still living in 1895 (Mell, 45). He and his second wife, Elizabeth Eliza Cooper, parented four sons and two daughters. Mell died at Athens, Georgia January 26, 1888 (*ESB*).

BIBLIOGRAPHY

2000 Annual of the 2000 Southern Baptist Convention. Nashville, TN: Executive Committee, Southern Baptist Convention, 2000.

Cathcart, William, ed. *The Baptist Encyclopaedia: A Dictionary of the Doctrines, Ordinances, Usages, Confessions of Faith, Sufferings, Labors, and Successes, and of the General History of the Baptist Denomination in All Lands, with Numerous Biographical Sketches of Distinguished American and Foreign Baptist, and a Supplement.* Philadelphia, Louis H. Everts, 1881; reprint, Paris, AR: Baptist Standard Bearer, 1988. 777.

Encyclopedia of Southern Baptists. S.v. "Mell, Patrick Hues," by Howard P. Giddens.

Mell, P. H. *A Southern Baptist Looks at Predestination.* [With a foreword and outline by Tom J. Nettles.] [Originally *Predestination and the Saints' Perseverance, Stated and Defended from the Objections of Arminians, in a Review of Two Sermons, Published by Rev. Russell Reneau.*] N.p.: ca. 1850; reprinted Cape Coral, FL: Christian Gospel Foundation & Pompano Beach, FL: North Pompano Baptist Church, N.d.

Mell, P. H. *Life of Patrick Hues Mell by His Son.* Louisville, KY: Baptist Book Concern, 1895.

BY JOHN FRANKLIN JONES
CORDOVA, TENNESSEE
JUNE 2004

THE BAPTIST STANDARD BEARER, INC.

a non-profit, tax-exempt corporation
committed to the Publication & Preservation
of the Baptist Heritage.

CURRENT TITLES AVAILABLE IN
THE BAPTIST *DISTINCTIVES* SERIES

KIFFIN, WILLIAM	A Sober Discourse of Right to Church-Communion. Wherein is proved by Scripture, the Example of the Primitive Times, and the Practice of All that have Professed the Christian Religion: That no Unbaptized person may be Regularly admitted to the Lord's Supper. (London: George Larkin, 1681).
KINGHORN, JOSEPH	Baptism, A Term of Communion. (Norwich: Bacon, Kinnebrook, and Co., 1816)
KINGHORN, JOSEPH	A Defense of "Baptism, A Term of Communion". In Answer To Robert Hall's Reply. (Norwich: Wilkin and Youngman, 1820).
GILL, JOHN	Gospel Baptism. A Collection of Sermons, Tracts, etc., on Scriptural Authority, the Nature of the New Testament Church and the Ordinance of Baptism by John Gill. (Paris, AR: The Baptist Standard Bearer, Inc., 2006).

CARSON, ALEXANDER	Ecclesiastical Polity of the New Testament. (Dublin: William Carson, 1856).
BOOTH, ABRAHAM	A Defense of the Baptists. A Declaration and Vindication of Three Historically Distinctive Baptist Principles. Compiled and Set Forth in the Republication of Three Books. Revised edition. (Paris, AR: The Baptist Standard Bearer, Inc., 2006).
BOOTH, ABRAHAM	Paedobaptism Examined on the Principles, Concessions, and Reasonings of the Most Learned Paedobaptists. With Replies to the Arguments and Objections of Dr. Williams and Mr. Peter Edwards. 3 volumes. (London: Ebenezer Palmer, 1829).
CARROLL, B. H.	*Ecclesia* - The Church. With an Appendix. (Louisville: Baptist Book Concern, 1903).
CHRISTIAN, JOHN T.	Immersion, The Act of Christian Baptism. (Louisville: Baptist Book Concern, 1891).
FROST, J. M.	Pedobaptism: Is It From Heaven Or Of Men? (Philadelphia: American Baptist Publication Society, 1875).
FULLER, RICHARD	Baptism, and the Terms of Communion; An Argument. (Charleston, SC: Southern Baptist Publication Society, 1854).
GRAVES, J. R.	Tri-Lemma: or, Death By Three Horns. The Presbyterian General Assembly Not Able To Decide This Question: "Is Baptism In The Romish Church Valid?" 1st Edition.

	(Nashville: Southwestern Publishing House, 1861).
MELL, P.H.	Baptism In Its Mode and Subjects. (Charleston, SC: Southern Baptist Publications Society, 1853).
JETER, JEREMIAH B.	Baptist Principles Reset. Consisting of Articles on Distinctive Baptist Principles by Various Authors. With an Appendix. (Richmond: The Religious Herald Co., 1902).
PENDLETON, J.M.	Distinctive Principles of Baptists. (Philadelphia: American Baptist Publication Society, 1882).
THOMAS, JESSE B.	The Church and the Kingdom. A New Testament Study. (Louisville: Baptist Book Concern, 1914).
WALLER, JOHN L.	Open Communion Shown to be Unscriptural & Deleterious. With an introductory essay by Dr. D. R. Campbell and an Appendix. (Louisville: Baptist Book Concern, 1859).

For a complete list of current authors/titles, visit our internet site at:
www.standardbearer.org
or write us at:

he Baptist Standard Bearer, Inc.

NUMBER ONE IRON OAKS DRIVE • PARIS, ARKANSAS 72855
TEL # 479-963-3831   FAX # 479-963-8083
EMAIL: Baptist@centurytel.net   http://www.standardbearer.org

Thou hast given a standard to them that fear thee; that it may be displayed because of the truth. — Psalm 60:4

www.ingramcontent.com/pod-product-compliance
Lightning Source LLC
Chambersburg PA
CBHW032000080426
42735CB00007B/456